SHINE ON YOU CRAZY DAISY
- VOLUME 2

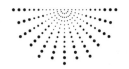

COMPILED BY TRUDY SIMMONS

THE DAISY CHAIN GROUP PUBLISHING HOUSE

CONTENTS

Printed in the United Kingdom
First Printing, October 2021

ISBN: 9781739914820 (paperback)
ISBN:9781739914837 (eBook)

The Daisy Chain Group International Ltd
Hampshire, UK
connect@thedaisychaingroup.com

Book Cover Design: Gemma Storey from Infinity Creative
Photo Credit of Trudy Simmons: Nisha Haq Photography

This book is dedicated to....

....All the businesswomen that are showing up and putting themselves out there to be seen and heard. We are all in this together... this is for you to take inspiration, that we are all on a similar journey, but taking different paths, with varying bumps along the way to here.

You can do it! Keep going!

ACKNOWLEDGMENTS

This is to acknowledge and appreciate all of those that have contributed and shared a piece of their journey with us all in this book. Thank you for your courage and tenacity. You are all inspirational.

There are wounds that get opened when you have your own business, and big conversations that need to be had around what you will stand for and what you will accept – OR NOT. I am so proud of all the brave and courageous women who choose to SHINE ON and use the big issues to create a better and bolder world for the rest of us to live in.

This is for the young woman that taught me that "practice makes progress" – and the fact that this is being taught in schools gives me hope for our next generation of entrepreneurs.

To the Facebook communities that I run – Hampshire Women's Business Group and International Women's Business Group for showing me each and every day that whatever we are going through, we are all there for each other. For being the communities that we all call "our lounge-room" where we come to share, ask for help, support, advice and give from our expertise without expectations. I am grateful for the "tribe" that we have and that like attracts like. Community is everything on this lonely road. Come and join ours, it is the best – tee hee!

I stand for inclusion on all aspects. The baseline of everything that we build is on kindness and being available with open arms to all businesswomen that wish to be a part of something and want to be seen and heard. We are here for all of that.

Welcome.

INTRODUCTION

This book is about creating a platform for businesswomen to have an inspirational voice and to share their stories with others, to show that this entrepreneurial rollercoaster is the highs AND the lows and that we navigate them all differently, but hopefully with a tribe/team of people that support our vision to our success – whatever that looks like, and it is different for everyone.

The stories were written in September 2021 – 18 months after Covid has hit our countries, our families and our businesses. Things are still raw, but the resilience is there!

Each story is unique, each story is REAL, each story offers a piece of insight, motivation and encouragement when we need it the most.

These are un-edited chapters of real stories from women that have been where you are and have stories to share about how to find your way, not feel isolated, find out what you CAN do, rather than feeling stuck in what you think you can't do.

Here…. Are their stories!! Bong bong…

Charity donation

As we gain, so can we give – that is my philosophy of running my own business. 10% of the profits from this book will be donated to the bereaved families of the NHS who have died while looking after us and our families during the Corona-Virus pandemic.

To find out more, or to donate, please visit this website – https://gofund.me/8aed0fc3

DO WHAT YOU LOVE; LOVE WHAT YOU DO

Trudy Simmons

We all, at various times in our lives, question just about everything we do! And when you're running your own business, those questions come thick and fast – daily, weekly, HOURLY sometimes!

We start our businesses wanting to make a difference – in our lives, in our families' lives and in the lives of our clients and audience.

We all know what we know, and we can do what we can do... I know... so deep....

Whatever we know and can do, we shouldn't lose sight of the fundamentals that we need to feel supported and like we can be functional human-beings. In business, I've found that these fundamentals are:

- Knowledge and learning
- Community and audience
- Tribe and support network
- Accountability and motivation

We make a difference in the services or products that we offer and how our clients value what we do. Whether you are assisting in curing cancer, fundraising for charity, offering a beautiful product, or teaching people yoga – you make a difference.

BUT… are you making sure that you are making a difference to yourself? Strange question, I know, but I spent the first few years of my business thinking that I knew enough to "get through", when actually, what I needed was a steady stream of new thinking, good people around me, and ways of going outside the box of what my business was.

Thought-provoking questions

Someone asked me a question after I'd been in business for about a year: "What difference are you making to your clients?" I could answer this question quite succinctly and with passion about the changes that I could see. I am a Clarity Business Coach, so being able to hear the change in how people talk about themselves and their businesses, especially when they have the "ah-ha!" epiphanies, is always a jaw-dropping-happy-dance moment. And when I could help clients who were willing to invest in themselves and their futures to see what they WANTED to do and WHY they wanted to do it, finding the direction and focus was a given. The big picture became clearer – wait for it…. The clouds parted and the sun shone – *cue the angels singing from above! The difference that I can make in helping them to have direction and focus gave me purpose in my business.

Then I was asked another question: "What difference are you making to yourself – AND – how are you going to make sure that you continue to make a difference to your life and those around you?" This was interesting and it made me stop, take stock, think, and make decisions. Without a doubt, I was making a difference, but what about the bigger impact? If I wanted to make a BIGGER difference and a BIGGER impact, what did I need to do, NOW? Don't worry, this isn't "answers on a postcard"; I'll tell you what I did.

I realised that to go bigger, I needed to keep learning, keep gaining knowledge from people who were further ahead in the journey than me, take on board the mistakes that they may have made and learn from my own mistakes, to make my business play bigger and not stay small.

Finding support

So the first thing that I did was join a business membership that taught us something new each month for us to implement.

The side-effect of joining this membership was that I found a tribe of businesswomen and a support network – and wowsers did I need that. You know the days when you're floundering? On those I'll literally be flopping around on the floor, throwing a tantrum, like a fish out of water (insert the visual here!). Having this support network was a game changer for being able to ask questions, see responses to other people's challenges and be taught to think outside the box to create more for yourself.

The next side-effect was getting accountable – now I am massively productive, and LOVE to help other people to be accountable to what they want to get done, but there is always that "secret list of things that you know you have to get done, but if you ignore it long enough, hopefully it will go away" – isn't there? (Please tell me you have this list too!?). So we started meeting up online or in-person (this was 10 years ago!) for working days. We were CRAZILY productive and supportive – hugely motivated, it was a win-win for us all in business growth. It gave us the opportunity to have dedicated time for working ON our businesses and not just IN them.

The other thing we all saw was that our audience grew, our community grew, the people who were drawn to our different personalities grew. We learnt more about personal branding and being the whole of yourself in your business than we had known before. Love what you do, do what you love – it makes a massive difference to what you create.

In the end, I think I was a member of at least four different business memberships to cover the fundamentals of what I needed so I could make sure I was building a sustainably-growing business – and why was I doing this? I wanted to always make sure that I could make a difference and impact businesswomen in a positive and motivating way.

Synchronicity

In 2016, I had been living in Australia for 15 years, I went over there for six months as a whippersnapper of 26, and 15 years later, I came back to the UK for a two-month holiday... and as before, I never went back.

It was a weird synchronicity of events that led to me having to pack up my house in the two weeks before I was leaving for my "holiday". Everything went into storage and a lot of my possessions just had to go. I sold my car "by accident" in that fortnight too – and then I boarded a jet plane to visit family and friends.

I was travelling with a friend, and I remember turning around to her after about a month away and saying, I'm not going home (to Australia); she didn't blink, she just said "OK" – and so the seed was sown.

At the time that I left Australia, I was questioning everything (again!). What was my business? What difference was I making?

Was it supporting me? Was I doing what I loved? Was I "successful"?

It all felt "too much", and I got to the UK burnt out, exhausted and ready to curl up in a ball and give up. But anyone who knows me, knows that I don't stay down for long, and like a child, I get bored quickly and need to feel challenged to find my va-va-voom!

After a month of travelling, my cupeth-were-filleth, so to speak, and I felt ready to ask myself the same questions as before, but with the intent of deciding what to do about the answers.

I looked at the business that I had created in Australia (and run successfully since 2010) and gave myself a little talking to – did I still want this? And the answer was a resounding YES! But then all the other questions came in – How? When? What? My Why has always been solid, I want to create safe platforms for business-women to be seen and heard (umm... look at these books and the accompanying podcast – my "why" is right there) – but also, I want to earn a shed-load so that I can give a shed-load away to charities and invest in the future development of young entrepreneurs.

So, I came back to my fundamentals of being a functional-human-being-in-business. I needed to find my tribe, my support network, my community. I needed to find new chal-lenges, new people who challenged me and new business-women to look up to. I needed to find resources for my continued learning and the places to go for those "yeah, but this just happened, what do I do now?" moments.

Creating what I needed

As with everything I do, if I can't find it, I create it, and that is what I did!

I wanted to make a difference locally first, and to meet

people "in-person-and-everything". So I set up a networking event to see what would happen. Quite wonderfully, four local businesswomen came along for a coffee and chat. I left there doing the proverbial cartwheel along the road, which is how I still feel about networking now, the BUZZ and motivation is business-affirming.

Then the wheels started turning. I set up a Facebook group to invite local businesswomen to advertise their products and services. I set up a regular monthly networking event, and within four months, I had 45 women turn up at a little local café – it was overwhelming, and so exciting that I couldn't shake the happy smile from my face for days.

But the local café said, "too many, split it, or change the venue". So I ended up setting up nearly 6 events per month in different areas locally. All of the events were selling out, all of the women had stories to tell, information to share, relationships to build and advice to ask for. Everyone knew that if they came to a Crazy Daisy Networking event, they would have fun, have a laugh, meet a beautiful bunch of businesswomen and exchange thoughts, ideas, talk about their businesses and do BUSINESS.

It was happening… it IS happening. Nothing changed during the craziness of 2020–21. We took everything online and the feeling is the same: business, sharing, giggle-snort, business, recommendations, giggle-snort, conversations; leave feeling motivated for the future, buzzing for the day – who needs coffee (well, me… don't take that away from me – tee hee).

Within 4 years of leaving Australia, in what felt like the strangest of synchronicities, but all for the right reasons, that initial need and want to build the business is and was still there.

I have built engaged and supportive communities (Hampshire Women's Business Group and International Women's Business Group). The Crazy Daisy Networking happens 4–6 times a month online and is available worldwide, to meet, interact, engage, and share with businesswomen we would NEVER have met before. The Spectacular Business Symposium is now online and can be viewed by its attendees all over the world, sharing the knowledge, expertise, and actionable steps to help us to grow and scale our businesses.

Sometimes, it is hard for us to admit to ourselves, and even more to others, the good that we do with the products and services we offer.

Do I love what I do? Yes, I absolutely do.

Do I make a difference? Yes, I hear that I do. Do I make a difference or a bigger impact for myself? I do, but I am always striving to learn more and do more to give us all the confidence to be the functioning-human-beings-in-business we want and deserve to be.

BIO:

Trudy Simmons is a Clarity and Productivity Business Coach for women entrepreneurs, with a truckload of empathy and a little bit of hard-arse!

She helps you find out WHAT you want to do, WHY you want to do it, and HOW to get it DONE!

She loves to show her audience how to become more successful by getting clarity, taking action and following through. Trudy has 20 years' experience in helping people move from being stuck and not knowing the next step, to getting their shizzle DONE by finding and harnessing their strengths and removing their weaknesses!

She knows what keeps you up at night – the thousand ideas that are germinating in your brain – and she knows how to sort them into "no go", "maybe later", and "hells yes", and get done what is really important to your success.

She is the creator and founder of: the Shine On You Crazy Daisy membership, The Crazy Daisy Networking Events, The Accountability Club, The Spectacular Online Business Symposium, The Spectacular Challenge to £1 Million, and The Happy Business Mastermind.

www.thedaisychaingroup.com

LESSONS FROM THE HEART

Gill Smith

D o you ever get that feeling that you are stuck? That somehow you're destined for more? You can't quite put your finger on it, but you know that the humdrum routines and treadmills simply aren't making your heart sing anymore?

Maybe you survived a traumatic experience and have a story to share?

Or maybe something happened in your life and you don't quite know the next steps to take, but somehow you trust that your intuition will guide you?

And maybe all that stuff you are going through or went through, has been gifted to you as an opportunity to change your life path and be, do and think completely differently about your goals, priorities and dreams?

What if all those things that happened, were simply meant to be?

What if, whatever brought you to this point, it boils down to having the courage to just *follow your heart?*

Back in 2015, I was a deputy headteacher in the largest high school in Lancashire. With 21 years experience in secondary teaching and over 15 years in senior leadership, I had the headship qualification and was ready to take on my own school.

I was the epitome of the career ladder.

Go to school, work hard, get good grades, head off to uni and get a good job, preferably one with a decent salary and pension, show up, go the extra mile, get promoted, work your way up, keep working hard, keep heading on up...

And so it went on.

For 21 years. All the while juggling motherhood, moving up the property ladder, relishing the fancy holidays, managing all of the things and 'having it all.'

Until our old friend, the universe, decided otherwise and intervened.

Intervened with one heck of a big bang.

Struck down with a sudden, critical level heart attack at the age of just 43, I was sick. Very, very sick. Panic spread through critical care as the busy cardiac team mopped up a distressed, scared and incredibly fearful Gill.

A few days into my stay in the cardiac unit, my favourite nurse took time to sit and wipe my tears. The tears of angst and upset; the questions and 'unanswerables' about *why me?* And with that, her words still burn deep in my soul:

"We're seeing more and more women like you here. Busy professional women juggling huge commitments. It's becoming normal. You need to seriously change your lifestyle if you want to live the rest of your life in good health and with happiness."

Those words cut deep.

And with no family history, arterial blockages, weight issues or other explanation, the trigger for the heart attack was...?

Stress.

Complete burnout.

A coronary artery spasm that could happen to any of us at any time.

Triggered by a multitude of possibilities, but notably a cocktail of adrenaline and cortisol, high beyond measure. Who knew that this could even happen? Living in a heightened state of red alert for years. Living in a heightened state of 'busy' and never really taking a break. Living in a heightened state of superwoman pushing through the symptoms and ailments including adrenal fatigue, pre-diabetes, migraines and labyrinthitis.

All that stuff I chose to ignore.

But hey! I was ever present at work. Never took time off. Didn't "feel stressed".

I'd been living a life of head buried in the sand, chasing career status and forgetting to prioritise self-care or consider the impact on my young family.

And so, after a long recovery and the bold decision to turn my back on stability and the pension, I left teaching.

I tuned into my heart.

Scared stiff about all that 'life stuff' like paying the mortgage and how would we afford the bills, I fought the sensible head demons, placed my trust in me and *put faith in my heart.*

I set about on a journey of learning, undoing old patterns, studying all things women's wellness, re-training in mindfulness, NLP, holistic therapies and nutrition coaching.

In 2016, I established my first business. A holistic therapy room offering therapeutic massage treatments and mindfulness, predominantly to stressed out women. Relatable.

The stressed out women started to bring their stressed out children along and combining my teaching experience with mindfulness and anxiety management, I helped families reduce stress and beat mindset gremlins with simple breathing techniques and relaxation.

Things really took off, word spread and before I knew it, I was speaking on stages and in businesses and organisations across the UK about the very, very real dangers of stress. Public speaking and consultancy work came naturally to me as a former teacher, and I embraced the chance to share my story in a bid to help other women understand the *very real* dangers of stress and burnout.

You see, there's something really important that you need to understand:

I'm not your stereotypical heart attack patient. Whatever that image conjures up for you!

Only four months before the 'event', as my cardiologist calls it, (as if it's some sort of great party that you planned for months, inviting all your friends along); I completed my first 5K park-run. I swam regularly. I clocked well over 10,000 steps a day patrolling those corridors and playgrounds of the high school.

I thought I was well.

But that's just it. We like to think we are doing all the right things.

And we often ignore the crucial signs from our very own heart!

Hindsight is a wonderful thing.

Trusting my heart, I started taking the mindset element of my work with young people online working predominantly with competitive swimmers – thanks to my connections and experience as a former swimmer and coach.

And ever thankful for my intuition, *I also felt my heart calling* to tackle the bucket list; writing two Amazon sports humour bestsellers in aid of The British Heart Foundation, alongside a range of tees, hoodies and totes.

Fast forward a few months.

Covid hit.

Pools closed. Competitions stopped. My businesses were grounded.

And with the overnight full stop imposed on me, *I drew confidence from my heart.*

I began to collaborate and in June 2020, forged a great partnership with Kate Offord; a swim and triathlon coach whose skills fully complemented mine.

Providing lockdown support for sporty teens and their mums, together we welcomed new clients and gave them a voice.

And there it was.

A sense of frustration and upset, as the mums grappled with Covid fears and disrupted sports and schooling.

As the women reached out to us, and to each other, the topic of conversation was changing. No longer just about the children, but conversations about their own personal wellbeing and mental health.

Their struggles and their fears.

We tuned into their hearts.

By listening to our invested audience, we had an epiphany moment.

We knew that any good business owner puts their customer first.

Our customers, these struggling mums, were signaling that it was time for us to lead them to step along a new path of managing their wellness and personal development.

By October 2020 we had launched an exclusive eight-week transformational life and wellness coaching programme for women.

We filled it within a week. Ten incredible women ready to rediscover their true self, uncover their blocks, understand the simple keys to wellness and make the change; however large or small.

We threw ourselves into the work.

And with it, the women started to experience phenomenal transformation in health, career, family life and personal goals.

And with it too, our confidence grew.

By January 2021, we delivered our first virtual sell-out retreat, and launched two more offers:

A well-priced, accessible wellness membership, **The Wellness Club,** for women needing support with all things eat – sleep – breathe – move, AND a six-month mastermind.

To say we got busy is an understatement.

But that's just it isn't it?

None of us came into business to be 'busy'.

Ever mindful of 'that' conversation with the cardiac nurse, the 'busy-ness' was not part of the new life plan.

We came into business to live calm and fulfilled lives on our own terms, to protect our health, to have more freedom over our time and to prioritise our families.

Ambitious, driven and focused, we felt we were losing sight of some of the very reasons we were doing this in the first place.

Our original purpose: Sharing our teachings and experiences with gentle and motivational support. To help women *follow their hearts* to reclaim health and happiness. To tune into their values and beliefs.

So we stopped and *listened to our hearts.*

And as if by magic, the universe took charge and intervened again.

Kate's life took a new turn as an incredible opportunity in the swim world materialised for her.

An opportunity too good to refuse that led her to make the huge decision to step away from the business and follow a new direction.

Incredibly brave and with my absolute support: *Trusting her heart.*

And so with deep trust, *I'm guided by my heart again.*

Moving into the next phase of business with nothing but gratitude.

Full circle back to where I started after the heart attack.

Simplifying. Streamlining. Reflecting. Taking breaks. Making time to flourish. Celebrating small wins. Moving forward.

Replenished.

I still have ambitious plans. But I'll never choose a life fuelled by a combo of caffeine, back to back appointments, a lack of boundaries and a depleted sense of who I really am like the bad old days!

Going back solo, I'm back in a position to *choose my heart's desires* and continue to do business differently.

And in all of this, I truly hope you will do the same.

Because life is precious.

It literally hangs by a thread.

When I woke up in the cardiac unit, I vowed I would never put work above my family ever again. I promised myself that I would always *believe in my heart.*

And the lessons?

Recognise that it's essential to stop.

Recognise that it's essential to breathe.

Recognise that it's essential to take the time to acknowledge just how far you've come.

Recognise that bumps in the road help you re-calibrate.

Recognise and celebrate the wins!

Know in your heart to prioritise yourself first.

Earlier in this chapter, I wrote this line:

"We knew that any good business owner puts their customer first."

I wonder how many of you questioned this when you read it?

Of course client satisfaction is key and I pride myself on making every person in my world feel noticed, valued and special.

But here's the thing:

"In truth, any good business owner should put themselves first."

And that's what I'm here for. It's my purpose.

To remind you. To guide and support you. To share perspective on the reality of burnout. To steer you to a path of high energy and wellness. And to help you stop ignoring the signs *to follow your heart.*

Perhaps you're reading this and thinking you may love to work with me. Or maybe you have it all under control and are already living a business life of 'unbusy.' (I applaud you!)

Whatever you take from this chapter, remember this:

With all the striving and ambition, you're no good to anyone burnt out.

Remember: Don't forget to make time for your wellness... or else you'll be making time for your illness.

Wishing you health and happiness.

From the bottom of my heart.

BIO:

Gill Smith of Gill Smith Holisitc Health helps women in their 40s and beyond to feel good about themselves again, regain energy and reclaim their health and happiness.

Creator of The BRAVE Method®, Gill supports professional and busy women with her simple EAT – SLEEP – BREATHE – MOVE framework for change.

Gill is 49 and is an award-winning teacher, nutritional and holistic therapist and mindset coach. She is now a passionate advocate for women's wellness following her recovery from a shock, out-of-the-blue heart attack in 2015.

@gillsmithholistichealth

3

LETTING GO OF "THE DREAM" TO
CREATE MY DREAM

Carol Perez

It's 2019; I'm at home, finishing a call with a client in Germany. I'm the Director of Operations of EMEA, a consulting company, and I work remotely. I'm a Mexican who's about to become British by choice. From the outside everything looks great. I moved to the UK seven years ago without a job and just one suitcase that could hold all my belongings. Slowly but surely, I'd managed to get my ideal job, and I'm in a flat in central London with two bedrooms and a terrace. I've done it! I'm living a "dream life" – but it's not my dream.

From the day I graduated, I dreamt about becoming a Director. I wanted to earn that title. I wanted to feel respected and accomplished. In 2011, I was living in Mexico with a great job, a great car, and I was the happy owner of a flat in the city centre. I "made it". I had a perfect life, married and accomplished! Everything looked great from the outside, but the reality was that we were bored. My husband (who is my best friend) and I had an honest conversation and realised we weren't made for settling. That afternoon we decided to embark on an adventure that changed my life. We decided to move out of Mexico. Our number one choice was London. I was obsessed with it. The year before we'd visited as tourists and I decided I wanted to live there. When? I didn't know, but I knew it would happen one day. That "one day" happened exactly a year after we visited as tourists.

We arrived with almost nothing. We bought a suitcase each, a limited number of Mexican Pesos (which converted to pounds are crumbs) and lots of expectations. We had an agreement; my husband would study, and I'd bring the money. It sounded more straightforward than it was.

For the first time in my adult life, I was jobless and felt lost without a job title. It wasn't easy to get a job, and I started to struggle. While I was trying to find one, I realised that my management role in Mexico meant nothing in the UK. I learnt how difficult everything is when you don't have a network. I discovered I was being judged because of my accent and my heritage. I found that not having access to the lifestyle I had in Mexico made me feel insecure. I realised that without my family, friends, and lifestyle, I felt lost. I didn't know who I was.

Who was I without a support network, retail therapy and fancy dinners? Who was I without a job? I started to feel I was made to do more. I began to believe that I was meant to do something bigger, something meaningful. But I ran out of time and intention. I got a job, and I started to feel comfortable again. I knew that way of living. I began to build relationships once again. Income wasn't a problem anymore and life was good. I felt like "myself" once again! Everything went back to "normal".

Legacies

By 2014, I was the Director of Operations for EMEA, a

consulting company. It was September when I heard the news. Gustavo Cerati passed away. If you had grown up in the 80s in Mexico, you'd have known who he was. He was an Argentinian composer, singer and songwriter who left an important legacy in how rock music evolved in Latin America. He impacted millions of people, and I was one of them. When he passed away, I started to question (once again) how I was living my life.

I asked myself, what would happen if I died tomorrow? What impact am I creating? What's my legacy? I realised that my death would impact loved ones, well, hopefully, haha! It would shock a couple of people, but that was it. I'd leave without impacting anybody else. My existence would be soon forgotten. I'd leave this planet worse than I found it, and I wasn't ready to accept that as my reality. I decided to do something about it! That year I decided to do things differently. I didn't know how or when but I wanted to do something to build a better world. Back then, I didn't realise how much inner work I'd need to do before attempting to create impact. At that moment, I didn't even know how much my "dream life" was based on someone else's dreams.

Finding my voice

I grew up in Mexico, a place where, sadly, femicides are common. It's also a country where you have more opportunities to succeed in anything you try if you are white or wealthy. Being a brown woman in my own country influenced my lack of confidence and self-expression. After doing a deep analysis and talking with friends about this, I decided to become a life coach. I wanted to support women to find their voice. It was 2015 when I got a certification. I designed a website, came up with a funky name and did everything "by the book" to build a successful business. However, nobody told me that I needed to develop a strong mindset and overcome many limiting beliefs.

To be frank, it was a comfortable side hustle. I had lots of clients, but I wasn't good at charging. I wasn't taking myself seriously because I didn't believe in myself. I was helping others to do what I couldn't do, finding my voice.

By 2019, my husband and I decided to leave our well-paid jobs and launch a business together. Tired of the negative publicity that Mexico has, we decided to do something about it. We launched a travel company to show people the beauty of Mexico City & Oaxaca. I was still "playing" to be a life coach, but now I was also the co-founder of a business that NEEDED to work because savings aren't infinite, right? Long story short, 2020 came to show us that launching a travel company was our biggest mistake but leaving the corporate job was our best decision ever. I decided to focus on my life coaching business. He decided to launch a sustainable streetwear brand. I was once again trying to build a business without doing the inner work.

May 2020 arrived, and, for the third time, I was reminded that I needed to do more. Unless you live under a rock, the name George Floyd will sound familiar to you. His death moved my world and so many other people's lives. It was the last call to do something different, and this time I took it seriously. In the weeks that followed, I witnessed how this event impacted and was approached by the people I admire and follow. Sháá Wasmund is one of them (if you don't know her, ask Google, she's fabulous!). I saw her genuinely interested in making a difference. I saw her concerned and busy redefining everything about her business. She wanted to build a bigger table, and she was looking for a Community Manager who was genuinely interested in inclusion, people, connection and business. Something about that post made me apply. I wasn't looking for "a job", but I knew I needed to do this. I could feel it. It was the time to allow The Carol Perez to awaken and take responsibility for herself and her dreams.

· · ·

The magic of community

It's been over a year since I applied for that job. Sháá is still my client, and I'm fortunate enough to call her my friend and mentor. Everything that has been happening since that day has been pure magic. I realised I LOVE building communities. I finally understood the meaning of the old saying, "do what you love, and you'll never work a day in your life".

I launched a business dedicated to helping changemakers to build thriving online communities that are also diverse and inclusive. I decided to make this business work, and that meant doing intense inner work to build up my confidence, overcome money mindset blocks and show up for me and my beliefs. I realised that to make a difference in this world, I needed to do things differently. I still want to support women to find their voice, but I realised that being a coach is not the only way to do it. There are many other ways to make that happen.

I've been working with amazing women, leaders in their industry who are looking to create a better world. For the first time in my life, I can see how my skills fit together beautifully. I spent more than 15 years in consulting and worked for Accenture for more than seven years; the skills I learnt through that work help me support others with strategy and processes to make their vision a reality.

As a consultant, I'd worked from home for more than eight years. During that time, I oversaw the operations of a team spread all over the world. That taught me how to connect, communicate and create a community regardless of location or time zone. I worked as a life coach for more than five years, which taught me to listen, connect and provide practical tools to help others to succeed. Oh! And I love technology; I have a degree in IT. Everything I've done so far has helped me create a business that fulfils me and is helping other business owners make this a better world. I'm The Carol Perez, and I'm here to help business owners create thriving, diverse and inclusive memberships and online groups.

Community is the future of business. Let's co-create online spaces where people feel seen, heard and included! Now, more than ever, the customer has a voice; magic happens when we provide platforms for them to connect and pursue a collective goal. This is me, this is my story, and I'm determined to change the world.

BIO:

Carol Perez is a community strategist who is passionate about helping changemakers create diverse and inclusive online spaces that support their vision and business goals. She's an expert in strategy, processes and community because of her 15+ years of experience in the consulting world. She's wonderful at connection and human behaviour because of her 5+ years of experience as a life coach. She has supported many business owners to build engaged communities, grow their audience and create an online space that works for them. When people feel seen, understood and supported, they open up and connect easily!

www.thecarolperez.com

THE WINDING PATH TO FREEDOM

Kate Powe

A s a five-year-old, I was quite adamant that when I grew up, I was going to be a nurse and a mother.

The moment I finished uni, already bitten by the travel bug, I was at the airport, desperate to start my year-long adventure around the globe (I didn't even wait for my own graduation.)

But as I moved into my early twenties, the drive for business success became my focus, and my idea of success looked like a big fat pay cheque with a large corporate. If I was associated with corporate success, then I would be successful.

And truth be told, if I had a superpower back then, it was nailing corporate interviews. I loved them. Oddly, it was the one area in my life where I truly felt a sense of utter confidence and self-belief.

So, I reached for the companies and industries in which I wanted to work: The largest global software company; A major investment bank; Australia's largest advertising agency, and I nabbed them all.

But gradually through each shiny new industry, company and position, the glow began to fade.

Don't get me wrong, the software company was awesome, fun, and offered travel through the States in the era of grunge. And hanging out in Seattle, working on the inception of email by day while rocking with Mother Love Bone at night was pretty much my idea of heaven. But I was craving creativity. I started to develop a secret obsession with typography, old signage and design.

Time for a career change, I jumped headlong into the world of graphic design, landing a gig in the studio of a major advertising agency. The glitzy and creative world of advertising would surely satisfy my restless soul.

But once again, after years of stressful deadlines, long hours and continuous weekend pitch-work, which often consisted of overnight sleep-overs on the studio floor, I was again left facing a familiar brick wall, re-questioning my life's purpose.

I continued on a series of career changes and challenges, but ultimately, all left me feeling like an exhausted cog in a wheel. I was playing the game and following a path I thought I wanted, but ultimately, my hunt for purpose and passion was leading me further from peace and personal satisfaction. I felt the pull for something more, but I still had no idea what that was or how to figure it out, let alone how to get there.

It was during this time that a long-term health struggle with my cycle amped up and became unbearable. As my stress increased, so did debilitating pain, flooding and crushing mood swings. I was jumping from doctor to doctor trying to find out what was wrong. I was prescribed multiple versions of the Pill and other hormones, none of which helped. Then I was recommended IUDs, anti-depressants, an ablation and a hysterectomy, the thought of which plummeted my heart further. I often couldn't get out of bed with pain. Personal plans, holidays, travel were frequently cancelled because I couldn't leave the house. I was taking more and more sick leave and ladling a whole heap of guilt on top of my physical pain. Eventually, through a chance appointment with a savvy GP, I was diagnosed with endometriosis and adenomyosis. These diagnoses really started the shift in my life trajectory. While it still took several years, alongside multiple surgeries, I knew I had to prioritise myself over the endless demands of clients and companies' bottom lines. I wanted to understand how my body ticked and I became deeply interested in how I could heal my body to stop the endless cycle of surgeries. And it sparked a new exploration into the world of energy healing and natural medicine.

Not to do things by halves, I packed up my apartment and moved myself to the "hippy" town of Byron Bay in Northern NSW. Here, I thought, I would find my home.

And I jumped in, feet first and way beyond my personal zone of comfort. I explored movement meditations including Five-Rhythms, Chakradance and Shaking (yep, it's a thing); crystal healing and psychic development; yoni healing, lomi lomi and shamanic work. I even embraced a ten-day silent retreat with devotees of Osho/Bhagwan Shree Rajneesh (a story in itself).

But after ten months of spiritual-searching, I was no closer to finding me. All I felt was the same sense of restlessness and a deep need to keep moving, exploring, searching. So once again, I packed up my home and returned to Sydney where I began to realise no matter how long my personal winding road, nothing is ever lost and there are no wrong turns.

I dove headlong back into study. First kinesiology, then naturopathy. I worked part time, studied full time and became increasingly fascinated by women's health. I loved the study, I loved having my brain active again, I loved the science, and I loved the meld with natural and energy medicine.

I pushed through my studies in record time with a triple workload and landed what I thought would be my dream career in a cutting-edge naturopathic clinic specialising in methylation and genetics.

But several months in, the continued pressure and stress I felt working for someone else left me feeling just as desperate as I had been back in corporate. I couldn't believe I'd been through all this change only to find myself repeating the same old pattern, feeling as overwhelmed and dissatisfied as before.

In a period of near-breakdown, I was forced to take a serious look at where I was and why I was there (again!). And through that process, I realised the change of jobs, industries, even locations had left me empty because I was still chasing the perception of success and happiness, rather than understanding what success and happiness meant or felt like for me. I'd never truly allowed myself to dream-up my ideal life; one that would make my soul sing. So, I allowed myself to dream, visualise and feel into how I wanted my work and personal life to be.

I encourage you to let that dream map out for yourself too. Get a big piece of paper and mind-map out your craziest, wildest idea of the perfect life. Leave no stone unturned and don't edit until you've emptied all your desires onto the page.

Mine went a little like this: freedom; loads of international travel and wild adventures with friends/partner; a pet; autonomy and authenticity; answering only to myself; working online from my cosy home or around the world where I could drink tea and consult and write and work to my own rhythm; being of service in the healing field, merging science, nature and spirit – and no stress!

As my dream vision melded with every cell in my body, I felt lightness and joy engulfing the ball of stress I had become.

And so, I left the supposed dream career I'd worked so hard for, and with my trusty laptop, birthed my online naturopathy business.

Eight years on, I look back in gratitude every day for following my gut instincts and breaking the pattern from head to heart-based decisions.

Being guided by my internal barometer saw my body begin to heal and with that, I could travel for several months every year, all the while working and serving my dream clients in women's health across the globe via online appointments. By listening to my truth, it allowed me freedom and a lifestyle that inspired and fed me.

And even now in our Covid-infused world, where working online is the "new normal", my business model has continued to allow me to work unhindered. My travel wings may be clipped but I continue to serve my local and global clients online just as well in lockdown as in Italy (unfortunately without that stunning view of the Duomo).

And what of the preceding long and winding path that seemed to hinder my happiness for so long? Thanks to my personal health journey, I was able to deeply understand and craft my niche in women's health and go on to help other women around the world with their own hormonal issues. And thanks to my software, advertising and design background, I was able to navigate and design my own website, social media and marketing strategy. Even my dalliance in Byron Bay further honed my natural connection to spirit and ability to work more intuitively. Truly, nothing is ever wasted and even the longest and most winding paths can lead us precisely to where we're meant to be, with all the experience to help us blossom once we get there.

The joy of helping thousands of women, often in areas where medical support is not easy to come by, without leaving my home, still fills me with awe. I've continued to harness my intuitive abilities which allows an even richer layer and experience to the healing process and I've never had to stop working to fulfil my passion for travel.

My model may not be for everyone, but it is perfection for me. And while I never did become a nurse or a mother (except to a little imp of a blue-point Siamese), those clear desires all those years ago to care, nurture and heal did manifest in my own personally crafted way.

And I now understand that our soul's calling is always there, patiently waiting to be heard, acknowledged and expressed. We just need to follow the threads that fascinate, for it to weave us.

BIO:

Kate is a qualified, Australian-based Naturopath with a passion for helping women through the hormonal maze to create balanced and enriched lives.

By integrating evidence-based medicine with natural healing practices, Kate addresses the underlying causes of hormonal disruption and offers guidance, education and support through the healing process.

Kate holds a Bachelor of Arts from the University of Sydney and an Adv. Dip. of Naturopathy from Nature Care College.

She is a member of the Australian Traditional Medicine Society and regularly furthers her education in Naturopathic Medicine, with particular interests in Endometriosis, PCOS and Peri-menopause.

www.katepowe.com

5

IF YOU BUILD IT, THEY WILL COME

Naetha Uren

T he seed was planted to start my own business thirty years before it actually bloomed.

Becoming a Licensed Chemical Dependency Counsellor (Addictions Counsellor) feels like a lifetime ago, it was an extension of my own recovery, but I wasn't sure if anything would come of it.

I went on to have a successful business career in hospitality and accommodation management, **yet never felt truly fulfilled**.

Five years ago, my daughter hit rock bottom with her own addictions. She was a victim of domestic violence, her life was falling apart, and my grandson needed support; so, my husband and I quit our jobs and went to America. We put all of our stuff in storage and ended the lease on our house. We just didn't know what we would have to deal with when we got to America or when we would come back to England. We got on a plane and went to save my grandson and hopefully, my daughter. Along the way, I learnt that our entire family needed recovery as much as my daughter did. Families, friends and communities are impacted so much by substance use, and I found out there are opportunities for everyone to embrace recovery. So, I delved into a recovery community in Houston, Texas, where I found support, resources, and compassion.

I was introduced to recovery coaching.

Recovery Coaching set my soul on fire. It gave me a place to belong; where I could do more than ask questions. I could also be a mentor, resource, guide, even a friend. It's where I learnt there are many pathways of recovery. Recovery Coaching allowed me to combine my professional training as a counsellor, coach, and mentor using my lived experience to do something with meaning and purpose.

I will never forget the first day of the training. I had dropped my daughter off at residential drug rehab the day before! I couldn't have planned it; every fibre in my body questioned if I was doing the right thing by attending the training. I considered cancelling, wondering, who am I to be there? But they welcomed me, and I realised it was exactly where I needed to be that day, with people who focused on recovery and creating recovery communities. On day two of that training, I was sitting on the rooftop of the Houston Council on Recovery in downtown Houston; coffee in hand, watching the sunrise across the city skyline, and I knew that this was where my heart for people met my head for business. It felt like fireworks exploding within me and around me. I realised I could use this incredible lived experience alongside all my counselling and business skills to make an impact in others' lives. And I knew this is what I was meant to do. That seed I'd planted had begun to sprout, and when it was time to return to England, I was ready to pursue the concept of recovery coaching abroad. In the following months, as we settled in with three generations under our roof, it became clear how much we all needed to implement all we'd learnt in America about recovery coaching. I watched my daughter try to find recovery support, and saw her encouraged to use again in order to access services.

I watched as the services available to my daughter in England minimised her dreams and ambitions. I knew we needed recovery coaching more than ever. Initially, I was full of self-doubt, worried I'd need a more reliable paycheck. Security and stability for my family had become my priority. I needed to pay bills. I was in fear of doing something different and failing. So, I took a job for a recovery organisation where the CEO expressed belief in me and my vision.

But I think once I got in there, the manager and other employees saw me as a threat. They seemed to feel I was challenging their blueprint for recovery instead of exploring multiple pathways. Hence, they weren't interested in recovery coaching, and everyday became a challenge. Eventually, my manager hired another guy who was his best mate, and it became cliquey and nasty. Then one day, the best mate said to my manager, "You just need to tell her to get back in her box. This will never work. She's too American and she needs to understand her place.".

I was challenging their old way of thinking with something new, and I think that scared them. Some people think change puts their recovery at risk. And it doesn't. There's more than one path to recovery, but that wasn't a conversation that people were ready to have at the time. That one person, that one statement shut me down for six months.

I was so depressed and full of self-doubt. I was asked to understand what it was about me that was affecting the people who did not believe in me. I wondered if the others were asked the same question. I was left with no choice but to walk away from that role. Funny thing is, I was then asked back to deliver the same recovery coaching training and workshops on a freelance basis. It was awkward, going back to the same place, knowing that people didn't believe in what I was doing. But I chose to rise up and take this as another opportunity to share recovery coaching and become more resilient. I learnt that all the people who attended those workshops were inspired and wanted to learn more; they gave me hope.

Then all of a sudden, Covid happened. And somewhere in that bubble of us all living together, accessing online learning, figuring out a way forward and just taking action, the vision began to blossom.

Recovery Coaching had already impacted my whole family so personally, and I saw how it worked in communities in America, but there was nothing like this where we lived. My daughter and I began to train with an organisation in the USA. We dove into learning, made connections, and had relational building conversations. Things changed.

The CEO really engaged with us, and one day I messaged him and said, "People in the UK need this. Is there any way we can bring this abroad?"

And he said, "I believe in you. If you build it, they will come and we will help and support you." And again, I was encouraged by someone believing in me, in us. But even as my daughter and I started the necessary training, I felt a big dash of self-doubt. Again, I said, "I can't do this."

My daughter and I were in the backyard, and she said, "Mom, just give me thirty days. I'll do all the social media and everything I can to make this work. You can't quit until you give me thirty days." And so, I did, and between us we managed to start it.

Shortly after that conversation, a Facebook business group I belong to ran a challenge called "£2K in 2 weeks," and I decided I was going to do this. I was scared shitless, but I followed every step of the challenge. I didn't make the £2K, but I did learn a lot, and I got some people to take the course and give me feedback.

More importantly, it proved to me, yet again, that there was viability, as well as a model that we could develop. So, we figured out what worked and didn't work and fixed it. And then we did it again and then again and kept tweaking it. And nine months since our first student, we're about to hit our first goal with a hundred people attending our Recovery Coach Training! Three years after I dropped my daughter at rehab, we've combined three households from two countries. I like to say we have "something for everyone, aged 7–79." We now have a somewhat crazy, but imperfectly perfect intergenerational family in recovery all living together.

Alongside all the changes, the business we started allows my daughter and I to share all the gifts we received in recovery, as well as our skills, unique chemistry and lived experience.

It took one person's discouraging words to send me into months of depression and self-doubt.

It took one person believing in and supporting me, to inspire me to take action. Today we are growing, as a business, as a family and as a recovery coaching community.

BIO:

Naetha Uren runs the Recovery Coach Academy and creates a place to learn about recovery coaching and also to connect and collaborate with others. With a combination of credible lived experience and professional skill, we are able to provide a unique and valuable perspective. While also providing opportunities to engage, enhance and elevate recovery coaching. By supporting others to implement recovery coaching and create Recovery Coach Communities, we make a bigger impact. If you would like to learn more, or have a Recovery Ready Conversation, please get in touch.

www.recoverycoachacademy.co.uk

6

RIGHT PLACE, RIGHT TIME, OR JUST RIGHT BELIEF?

Suzy Dierckx

"What will you be doing after school?" she asked.
"I'm going to Great Ormond Street to train as a paediatric nurse", I said aged 13.

"What a wonderful profession", replied the Queen.

What an inspiring moment, the day I verbalised to Her Majesty Queen Elizabeth II at my secondary school in 1993 that I was going to be a nurse, one caring for vulnerable and sick children. That was my calling and my forever job, or was it?

Finding my place

Today I am not a paediatric nurse; however, I will never forget my heritage, my roots and the training that prepared me for the career that followed.

At university, I found my voice. My brain awoke with an inherent passion to study something that made me feel alive. Something that inspired me and equipped me with knowledge I still use today in my business. I loved what I did and truly felt alive, but I didn't always want to be available, not at the beck and call of the rota or someone else's agenda. Could I ever be free of that?

After my 3 year degree, I obtained a 1st class honours and was offered a PhD post. At the time I didn't realise the honour or even the direction that this would have taken me, but I declined. I thought I couldn't be a 'Dr' of nursing without having held a sick child's hand or two. Still, I had graduated and I was so proud.

A few years later I took a research trip to Dubai with a colleague, as we wanted to understand the difference in medical practices in the Middle East versus the UK. The trip was an eye opener. Not only from a cultural and healthcare perspective, but also the shiny world of corporate entertainment.

A healthcare company sponsored and chaperoned us around, entertained us and upgraded our grotty hotel. We were living a dream.

As I left Dubai, the CEO of a healthcare company gave me his business card: "Call me when you want a job".

Two years later, I made that call. I'd come to a crossroads in my career and wanted to make some life changing decisions. To teach nursing, manage nurses or pivot? I found 'my out', I chose pivot.

I spent 13 wonderful years at the Dubai healthcare company, having started in marketing. They said I was 'too green' for sales, but as my career developed, so did my business acumen. I was marketing to nurses, doctors, allied health professionals, and I could talk the talk.

I loved it, I understood it, and I flew. I equipped the sales teams with marketing collateral to help sell our products. I created campaigns to help market the products. I worked with global teams to develop the product pipeline, and I had 18 marketing colleagues across the globe who looked to me for help and advice. I felt empowered. I won awards, and I was respected and knowledgeable. I studied and backed the real life experience with a marketing qualification.

Then along came my family and something changed. Something had to.

Reality shifted

My focus on work and being at the beck and call of a large corporate machine was impacted by my responsibilities at home. I couldn't be at Heathrow at 5am, because who could look after my children at that time? I negotiated a 4-day week but on my third maternity leave, it really was crunch time. I jumped the Euro HQ boat and headed back to the UK shore where I started a training role. Deep down I knew the commute was still too hard and during a merger and acquisition, my role expired. P45 in hand, I skipped away leaving behind a large corporation to follow my own destiny. The hidden cloak of guilt for working late while ignoring a child or leaving work early to watch your child play in the ukulele concert at school, needed to be lifted. Everything felt like a compromise!

For years, my hubby and biggest cheerleader had been saying I should set up on my own. I had years of "You would be brilliant"; BUT I didn't believe it, and I wasn't ready until 2017.

After my third child, I knew I couldn't survive in the corporate world, as my responsibilities at home had changed. So I fled, I pivoted and followed my dream of a more flexible work-life balance.

I didn't want to be just a 'marketing consultant', so I had to think hard on how to utilise my skills and do something that I loved. I had to work flexibly for me and my young family. I felt scared but exhilarated. I was taking a leap of faith. I applied to 'digital mums' to retrain as a social media consultant. The 6-month course equipped me with the right skills (and polished a few) to set up on my own, and I haven't looked back. Running a social media campaign in and for businesses in Winchester helped me meet local clients/ contacts, which ultimately helped me start my business.

I am finally home

SociableSuzy is built upon my own values of honesty, integrity, and trust. I love working with businesses who share these values; they recognise my corporate heritage and drive, plus they love my human side. They respect the fact I am a working mum too, which is important. That hidden cloak of guilt has been locked away. Of course it comes out occasionally, but I have to make the choices now for when I need to be flexible with my working time. We are all people at the end of the day, and I choose when to work and with whom. That's so empowering!

As I sit and write this today, my business, SociableSuzy, is 3.5 years old. Working through the pandemic was hard, but I chose to retrain in something that met my objective to be a better working mum, and that's what I will always strive to be, as my young family grows. I juggled the kids around the home schooling efforts, and I worked flexibly with very understanding clients. I lost some but gained some on the way, too.

Communication has never been so important and I'm grateful to my training for providing solid foundations in that. I love to talk with people and actively listen. You can learn a great deal from that. My business today continues to grow and as my working time reduces and my offering adapts to help clients meet their requirements.

Building a business community

I enjoy sharing my skills with businesses that need them. In the first year I won a Hampshire Women's Business Award which recognised my desire to reach for the stars. Today I accept that my own success in business is through the efforts I put in, the connections I make, as well as the support I have been given and that I have provided others.

Networking was a big part of my business's evolution. I met local freelancers and SMEs through social media, connecting online and also face-to-face. I attended networking groups and met some truly inspiring people who had also taken the steps to becoming their own boss. Finding people who align with your morals has been important and those relationships I have invested in.

Being your own boss isn't easy. From accounts to sales to marketing to office cleaning – my head can be turned in many directions – but I call the shots. I screen who I work with and for, based on my gut, even today. Trust your instincts. They may not always be right, but it's a great place to start.

I love the ability to change my diary, the nature of my work is very flexible, and I love that ability to flex. I plan my workload around the family diary and am happy to work for myself. I gain a great balance from mix of visiting clients face-to face and online – something that I utilised even before the Covid pandemic. I love live events too and can't wait see them come back as the world hopefully recovers well from Covid.

When you first start a business, you realise that it's just you. There's no IT help desk or a tea lady: it really is all on you. However, you adapt and find comfort in learning new skills or outsourcing to an expert. There are also plenty of business coaches who can help if you need one. I found strength in making my own decisions, meeting new people locally and feeling my way. I also outsourced the things I knew would challenge me, or I didn't have capacity to learn well quickly, like accounting! I am truly grateful for the support of my accountant and her words of wisdom along my journey.

Learning experiences

It may not be for everyone, but my business has grown through making good and bad decisions. I also have a massive network of fellow 'digital mums' who keep me abreast of changes, current questions and are a huge support in my business field.

Early on, I said yes to most things but actually wished I hadn't. You know the style and character types of people that you like to work with. Some 'demanded' my time which felt icky at the time, and I wish I had declined to work with them, but you learn as you go.

Working with people I can motivate and inspire really makes me feel great! It's also lovely if they like to share a Coke Zero, slice of cake, and a giggle. You really should work with the people you choose. As we all know, people buy from people, so your gut instinct is usually right! (Cake really helps too!)

Running a business equips you with skills that you wouldn't believe. Multitasking plays a huge component in my work/life schedule. I make the decisions for the business, and I am proud to be generating great profit for a business that I mould around my other commitments. It is a business I am proud of, and I can't wait to introduce new products/services in the future that help meet my clients' needs. I am also hoping to launch a new business very soon too, which will also hopefully slot into an already busy schedule.

As well as my freelance work, I also sit comfortably under the wing of a local communications agency, and one day, I aspire to have a team of people working for me. For now, I'm happy, but who knows where the next few years will take us?

Sometimes it's not just the right place or right time but having the belief in yourself too.

My path thus far hasn't been straight, but I've loved every twist and turn. It's taught me I can do what I believe in and that every turn leads somewhere new. I hope this chapter has inspired you a little and wish you well on your chosen path!

BIO:

I'm Suzy Dierckx, founder of SociableSuzy. I am a social media marketing consultant, mum of three small people (plus a cute puppy), CEO of the home, and wife to my epic Belgian husband, living in the sunny suburbs of Winchester, Hampshire.

For my day job, I help SME's find their voice on social media and help them gain insights/experience or add a strategy to grow their online presence. I love teaching businesses new skills and helping them digest the ongoing evolution of social media through workshops or 1:1 bespoke sessions.

www.instagram.com/sociablesuzy

7

THE LEATHER JACKET

Karly Nimmo

M oney was flowing. My voice over agency was really starting to thrive after 3 years in. It was 2009 and though most of the global economy was turning to shit, business for me was booming. I was making more money than I ever had before, had little overheads and terrible skills at managing my finances. The business bank account was my bank account. There was no separation. My groceries were mixed in with business expenses. No tax offset account. No separate savings. Just money. My money.

I'd never been good with money. When I got my first tax return I spent every last cent on a CD disc changer stereo (which was the latest tech in 1992)). When I moved out of home at 18 I needed a bed, didn't have the cash, so I went and put one on 12 months interest free. 24 months later I'd never made a payment, and ended up paying ridiculous interest on that $500 bed. After all was said and done, with what I was out of pocket, I could have bought a more luxurious mattress topped Californian King, instead of my pretty standard inner spring queen. WTF?

These two events really highlight what were my two money operating modes: If I had cash I'd spend it as fast as it came in. And, when it came to my financial obligations, avoidance was my M.O.

One day, in the thick of my online shopping addiction, the parcel postie (who I was on a first name basis with) knocked on my door with yet another parcel. This time it wasn't a stack of macrame books from the 1970s, or a random mid-century statue, or some Mexican silver art deco jewellery. This time, it was my most extravagant purchase to date. A tan coloured $1500 D&G leather jacket – that was on special (that was my justification – it was a bargain at just $800).

I'm not sure what I was thinking when I bought it.

Actually, I do know what I was thinking when I bought it.

I was depressed, anxious and very lonely. I wanted to be ready to impress people with my designer label clothes, watch, sunglasses, make up, etc. It felt like all this stuff legitimised my success, and made me more interesting, or something. People would look up to me. Be impressed. Want to be my friend. People would think I was cooler than I felt. That I had my shit together. I'd be more legitimate as a human being.

On that day, as I stood in front of the mirror, with my expensive designer leather jacket on, I wasn't that impressed. But I couldn't admit that to myself. I bought it. I was committed. Returning something for a refund felt like it carried some kind of shame. So, unless there was a real reason for returning the jacket, like it didn't fit or it was faulty in some way, I'd have to keep it. I tried to imagine how others might see me in this jacket. Would I look cool? Like a success?

Part of me was let down that the jacket didn't do something really remarkable to me. I guess I was expecting to like myself, but there I was. Same old me. Just wrapped in a tan coloured, expensive leather jacket.

I took the jacket off and lay it neatly on the bed. Then I heard the familiar sound of the regular posties motorbike. The sound of his bike idling, the squeak of the letterbox being opened and closed and the putting as the bike moved on down the neighbourhood. Rev, screech, idle, putt. Rev, screech, idle, putt. Rev, screech, idle, putt off into the distance.

As I pulled out the mail, my mind was preoccupied with the jacket. I felt like a bit of an idiot. Angry at myself. Angry at the jacket. I mindlessly tore open the letters, one by one. Political marketing. Something from a new home charity raffle. A phone bill. Just the usual shit.

My stomach dropped as I opened the last letter. A tax bill from the Australian Tax Office (ATO). I was usually so adept at avoiding opening letters from the ATO. The jackets arrival had thrown me off my avoidance game. There was no hiding the news this letter contained by hiding it underneath a pile of unopened, unimportant mail. From my experience, letters from the ATO never contained good news. Just represented how shit I was with money.

This time was no different.

I owed the ATO $14,000... that I certainly did not have. I felt sick to my stomach. This wasn't the first time I'd found myself owing the tax office way more money than I had, and it wouldn't be the last time. Secretly, I knew this was coming. And I'd been pulling the ostrich move (burying my head in the sand and waiting for it to go away). I'd spent many sleepless nights in the lead up thinking about how and when this day would arrive. And now that it was here, my body had a visceral reaction to the news. Panic and dread and guilt and shame. All very familiar feelings.

There was no way in hell I could keep the stupid jacket. No

way. With a sense of shame, I carefully wrapped the jacket back in its fancy tissue paper wrapping, and took it to the post office to send back for a refund. Part of me was relieved it was gone. I knew a leather jacket was kind of ridiculous in the warm climate of the Mid North Coast of NSW of Australia; a place where I rarely wore shoes, let alone leather jackets! To be honest, that was part of the attraction: to have something expensive that rarely saw the light of day seemed to make it more extravagant.

Often we are told to 'stretch ourselves' and 'go splurge', – especially by those in the female entrepreneur world. We are told that the universe backs us, when we put our money where our mouth is and invest in things that we'd generally consider outside of our reach. It encourages frivolous spending and tells us that the universe delivers more to us when we act 'as if'. Well, I certainly acted 'as if' that day and it totally backfired in my face. In fact, most of the time when I've invested in something that felt like a huge stretch, it's not worked out to plan.

You maybe thinking 'oh Karly. That's just a limiting belief showing up'. And maybe it is. Yet I see it slightly differently.

Every time I've invested in something where the foundation has been based in fear (mostly of not being enough as I am), it's backfired. I've been left to clean up a financial, or emotional, mess. This leaves me feeling shit about myself, reinforcing the story that I'm not enough. A fuck up. A failure. Someone who doesn't finish anything she starts. Which is bullshit.

This is something no one really talks about, right? There is no way to buy yourself out of feeling shit about yourself. There's nothing you can buy that will be 'the one thing' to fix your shit. Those magic bullets to your ideal life (body, business, relationship, wealth, success, etc)… well, let's just say that I've never seen one work.

From my experience, It doesn't work that way. There's a process to things. And as much as someone can promise a 'roadmap' or 'blueprint' to what you want, there's really no skipping steps.

When we buy stuff from a FOMO (fear of missing out) place, we rarely move forward from where we are. Maybe we don't even use the thing, or get the most out of it, because it's somehow energetically attached to that feeling of not being enough. Therefore, our behaviour will reinforce those negative feelings; primarily aimed squarely at ourselves and our apparent 'not enough-ness'.

FOMO isn't just about missing out on an event. It's not just about missing out on that deadline, or that opportunity, or that thing. It's also about missing out on what we perceive we need to be/have/do in order to have/do/be *insert thing we want here*. I've seen first-hand from experience that when one does buy from that place, they rarely move forward.

But, when we buy from a place where we feel empowered and ready, change is pretty much guaranteed: with, or without, the thing we think we need. I'm constantly reminding myself 'what is for me, won't go by me'. We can't miss something that is destined for us. Now, I can't say that for certain. Perhaps, in the wise words of Dr Suess, 'And will you succeed? Yes! You will, indeed! (98 and 3/4 percent guaranteed.)'.

The leather jacket was never going to be the thing that made people see me in the light I wanted them to (successful). The leather jacket was just a tan coloured, nicely tailored Band-Aid to a much bigger issue, quietly lurking underneath my perfectly manicured hair and face. Let's face it, my shopping addiction was a symptom of a much deeper issue – my distinct lack of love and respect for myself.

It's not about the leather jacket being 'the thing'. I am the thing. You are the thing.

I was going to say that before others can see you as 'successful', you need to see yourself as 'successful'. Yet that's not true. Not at all. Right now, I can (again, 98 and 3/4 percent guarantee) that there are plenty of people in your life that see you in that light, right now.

But the only one that really matters... is you.

Remember that next time you find yourself on the checkout page for something you likely wouldn't need if you felt like you were enough.

BIO:

With five iTunes hit podcasts under her belt, including Karlosophies and Rock Your Mic Right, Karly Nimmo is all about voice. An experienced voice over artist, running her successful voice over agency since 2006, her clients include a very long list of Australia's largest brands and organisations. She's also taught and supported over 300 podcasters via her online podcasting programmes; Radcasters and Frequency. After over 15 years of business success, and plenty of failures, she loves to use her voice to tell a hilarious, and sometimes heartbreaking, tale or two.

www.karlynimmo.com

8

I JUST WANTED TO TAKE PHOTOS...

Suzy Ellis

I started my business for a combination of reasons. I'm a creative being and have always had a love for anything that gets my creative juices flowing. None of my previous jobs had done this, and professional photography was something I had been toying with for a few years. I invested in going back to college to train in the evenings while working my full-time job, but with the combination of paying my mortgage, the insecurity of not having a reliable monthly income and self-doubt, I had put off the idea of going into photography full-time. After being offered a promotion in my previous job, I decided to turn it down, despite the massive financial incentive as I realised that it would have made me miserable being stuck in a job I had no passion for. My husband and I have always been firm believers in happiness and life above career, and sometimes that has meant making sacrifices in terms of money, but ultimately it was the right decision.

After I had my daughter I had to make a choice between returning to work in order to fund childcare, or to be a full time mother. Sending my children to nursery is important to me as I personally think it is very good for their physical and mental development, but it is also beneficial to my mental health to have some time apart from them to be someone other than 'Mummy' for a few hours. I was able to work a part-time job in the travel industry with just my daughter, but once my son came along I had a choice to make. Either find a job which would fit around childcare, or take the leap of faith and start my own business where I could be in control of my own time and be my own boss. I talked it through with my husband and we came to the conclusion that I would give it a year and see how it went. Little did we know that Covid was just around the corner!

I can honestly say that when I started the business I was completely at sea. I had no idea what I was doing or how to set up and run a successful business! I offered portrait photography but with no niche or unique selling point. I made some very bad investments in the early days, for example, my website. I didn't look into branding or my ideal client and I didn't ask for recommendations or testimonials when choosing a web designer. I paid the price and it is a lesson I have learnt the hard way. I now always do my research before investing in anything for my business and make sure I'm investing in the right person for the right reason and that I am going to get a positive return on that investment.

For anyone looking to start their own business, my advice would be to invest in a course or mentor to take you through it step by step so you get it right the first time. Most people don't realise that becoming self-employed generally means that to start with you spend around 75% of your time running your business, marketing, planning, doing your finances etc. and the other 25% actually doing whatever it is you do.

Luckily I quickly came across an amazing mentor who had an online course with a step by step guide to set up and running a successful brand photography business. It was the best investment I could have made and has been the foundation of my business. I finally had some direction and a mentor to help me on my way. Brand photography was a game changer for me and everything kind of clicked into place. I loved the idea of helping other business owners, and while I didn't want to give up on portraits altogether, it allowed me to develop a niche and become a specialist in my area of photography. Helping other ladies to transform their business into something they are proud of is so rewarding! I love helping women who felt nervous to start with, as they begin to relax into the shoot and really enjoy themselves. It's the best feeling when they receive their completed gallery and fall in love with the natural-looking images. It gives me really high levels of job satisfaction, something I'd never have got if I'd stayed in my previous marketing role.

Then we went into lockdown.

Lockdown was tough. I'm not going to lie. I was in a very fortunate position where my husband, who is a key worker, was able to support both of us, and without having to pay nursery fees we managed to get by ok. However it meant that I became a full-time mum which is never something I had ever planned on doing. Looking back I can definitely see the benefits from that time. I actually really bonded with the children, and they bonded with each other. Don't get me wrong, it may have been a completely different story if the weather wasn't so nice and we hadn't spent most of our time in the garden, but we got by fine. From a business point of view I had to take a step back and think about how I could keep my business alive while not being able to go out for photoshoots. I spent a lot of time in the evenings focusing on networking, getting my name out and being active on social media. I ran a competition to build up a mailing list and develop some business for when restrictions were lifted. By the time lockdown was over I went into July with plenty of business to keep me going.

I am a part-time working mum, so my kids go to nursery two days a week and my family for another day which gives me 3 days to work, plus the weekend or evenings when needed. The amazing thing about brand photography is that it generally takes place during the week which allows me to be home with my family on the weekends. With young children that is obviously really important to me. However being a working mum with young children has its challenges. I am the one who has to be on call if one of them gets hurt or falls ill during the day. If they wake up with a fever then my work has to take the hit and I have to rearrange my schedule. When the nursery closed for 10 days due to the staff having Covid, work went out the window. That has been one of the hardest factors for me, but I have designed my brand around being a working mum and part of that does include the fact that unfortunately, sometimes things happen and I have to rearrange. Most of my clients are very understanding as they know who I am when they start working with me. The blessing with brand photography is, unlike a wedding, it can usually be rearranged fairly easily.

Working from home has also been another challenge. It took a while to get used to being alone and being strict on my working hours. It's very tempting to clear up the breakfast, hang the washing out, clean the kitchen, change the bedsheets and empty the dishwasher before sitting down to work, but if I did that then it would be lunchtime before I even started. I've had to compartmentalise my life to manage my time effectively. Housework doesn't get done during work hours. My husband has accepted that, and he's also had to learn this rule since he's started working from home occasionally.

Since I started the business I have learnt a lot of lessons. During lockdown I suffered with some pretty severe imposter syndrome. Looking at other photographers growing their businesses and doing everything I wished I could was tough. But I've come to realise that I am a part-time working mum and there is only so much I can do with my time. A combination of outsourcing the work that I hate (bookkeeping, some social media, my email marketing etc) has freed up my time to do more photography, and time management has meant that I only book in what I am able to do and not overwhelm myself. I am also always trying new things. I recently did some photography for my kids' nursery which I loved, so I am looking at possibly doing more of that in the future. Portrait photography is actually easier for me to market, as with two young kids I am constantly networking with my ideal client without consciously doing it.

My business is in a constant state of change at the moment. I am learning to balance the brand and portrait sides and what the best way to market them is. I specialise in brand photography but I keep my hand in with portraits by providing seasonal mini shoots four times a year and taking on a few bespoke bookings. I still have a long way to go in terms of getting everything together, but I'm very proud of what I've achieved in a couple of years. I have grown as a person and I have met some truly inspiring people recently.

I'm still fairly uncertain about where my business will go in the future, but I've started to think about what I want to do once both my children start school. Since starting my business it's always been a case of "when the kids go to school I'll have time to…." But someone asked me the other day if I actually want to work full time, or whether I might want to have a day just for me. I am still considering how I want the future to look and planning what I want to achieve. My big dreams include being able to afford to move house and have my own garden studio. But in the meantime I'm focusing on maintaining a healthy work/life balance for myself and my family while building a name for myself in Hampshire and Wiltshire as a go to Brand Photographer, and in Salisbury as a portrait photographer.

BIO:

Suzy Ellis is a Brand Photography Specialist based in Salisbury, Wiltshire, where she lives with her husband and two children. As a young adult she travelled the world, and capturing those fun-filled moments on camera, developed her love of photography. Suzy specialises in helping self-employed women in Hampshire and Wiltshire to bring their brand to life with a gallery of beautiful professional images to use throughout their marketing and social media. Suzy brings her happy enthusiasm to her work; photoshoots with her are a lot of fun so the smiles and emotions in her shots are totally natural. If she's not behind her camera or busy editing, you will usually find Suzy spending time with her family and friends enjoying good food and wine in the sunshine or playing a game of tennis.

www.suzyellisbrandphotography.co.uk

9

INSPIRED TO GO IT ALONE

Celia Clark

It's funny how throwaway comments can change the direction of your life. I'd spent 10 years inhouse helping people perform well and find satisfaction in their publishing jobs, when a colleague casually observed that I was a 'lifer' in the business. This opened a floodgate of questions for me: Did I want that? What was I shying away from by staying put? And the hardest question of all: what else did I want to do?

I enjoyed many aspects of my learning and development job but couldn't see myself moving to do a similar one elsewhere. My colleagues were lovely but internal politics was frustrating. The job fitted around my family but deep down I wanted to be home even more as they grew up. These deliberations revolved round my head like the wheels of my bike as I cycled home each day. I knew I was ready for a change but I was scared: scared I'd choose the wrong thing, that I'd be worse off not better.

However, three events over the next five years seeded a vague idea to 'do more with coaching', the bit of my job I loved best. I completed a postgraduate coaching qualification, the richest learning experience of my life. Feedback from my fellow coaches helped me believe that this was something I did *really well*. In 2015 I lost my mum to dementia but out of the sadness came the possibility of investing my inheritance in my next life step as a way of honouring and paying forward her love. Finally, I did a powerful visualisation on a leadership course during which I had to ask for the 'gift' I needed to succeed; I got a silver rod of courage. As strange as it sounds, it made a difference. I began pushing through my fears and discovered that it was actually quite exhilarating to do things that scared me!

The possibility that I could run my own business certainly felt scary but it intrigued me too. I'd seen the challenges of self-employment growing up in my family's busy Post Office. I knew about the long hours, that it's demanding to be jack-of-all-trades and daunting to shoulder responsibility. But there's the satisfaction of shaping something of your own making, the flexibility of deciding your hours and the relief of not having to seek someone else's approval on every decision.

Could I do that? Could I leave the safety of employment and stand on my own feet? That's when I realised I *wanted* to do this to prove to myself what I was capable of. I wanted to learn new stuff, confront my limiting beliefs and make a difference to people, because I *love* helping people recognise what they're good at and put it at the heart of what they do.

Take Lorraine for example, who I coached as part of a management course I co-led. Stepping back and reflecting objectively on her strengths opened Lorraine's eyes to her untapped potential. Recently I received a lovely email from her. It read: "You probably don't remember me but I remember you very well. You helped me to change my life. The coaching made me question myself and think about what I really wanted. Since then, I have achieved many new things including my first-class degree, running a global team and working in other countries."

I'd found my purpose. I wanted to bring this sort of insight and inspiration to lots of other people. I had the skills and experience I needed coupled with a strong conviction that women especially were too often hindered by things like imposter syndrome, fear of conflict and perfectionism. So in 2016, I handed in my notice with the intention of building a coaching practice aimed at helping women find happiness and success in their work.

It wasn't an overnight transition. I granted myself a gap year in which I relaxed, developed an enthusiasm for DIY and challenged myself to walk 1000 miles. I then started putting things in place: choosing the name Inspires Coaching (because I live in the dreaming spires of Oxford), getting insurance, creating my own logo. I did some gratis coaching to build experience of running a relationship from start to finish. The books say be wary of offering your services for free, but this was good learning and a confidence boost when they came back later as paying clients. Until I *had* some paying clients though, I cut back on personal spending and took a part-time job to cover my share of the bills.

I told myself and anyone who asked that things were building slowly but nicely thank you alongside my salaried job, but they weren't really. Some work found me, but I discovered I hadn't got the energy to hold down two jobs. I know people who do and I seriously respect them for it now but I've learnt to accept some limitations. Too much desk work leaves me with chronic back pain therefore working at a computer all day then coming home and switching on the laptop was not sustainable. I could commit to one or the other, but not both, and so I took the plunge to go solely self-employed from September 2019.

That upped the stakes but this commitment was the first game changer for me. Here are the eight others.

1. Discovering positive intelligence

Mindset is everything, or certainly a whacking big chunk of it! You have two voices in your head: the positive one, good at rational and creative thinking, and the emotionally-driven negative one, trying to keep you safe but ultimately holding you back. The one you listen to wins. In the techniques of positive intelligence, I've found simple ways to tune out the negative and access the positive. I feel more centred than I've ever been. I'm not slowed down by perfectionism and can talk about what I offer without feeling boastful.

2. Finding a 'guru' who speaks my language

A lot of advice I read suggested I could only succeed if I dedicated every hour of my life to my venture. So I was relieved to find the 'Chillpreneur', Denise Duffield-Thomas, whose take on business is who wants to get up at 5am when you were up at 4 with one of the kids! At last, someone who got my world. Reading and applying her advice has been practical and inspirational.

3. Reaching out for help

Business books are one thing but getting specific help with your own situation is invaluable. Despite knowing the benefits of coaching, those negative voices led me into the trap of thinking it would be an admission of failure to ask for help. I reached a point of real doubt that I could see this through before I booked some business coaching with Trudy Simmons. What a turning point! It was such a relief to get tailored support and gain a fairer perspective on how I was doing but it was more than that – it was the decision to take action to *invest* in myself that was hugely empowering.

. . .

4. Time blocking

One of my motivations for setting up my own business was to have more flexibility over my time but for the first year (which coincided with the arrival of Covid and the rest of the family invading 'my space'!) this meant I didn't commit to regular hours. Trudy highlighted this paradox and introduced me to time blocking: scheduling specific times for specific activities. My week is now divided into times for meeting clients, marketing, learning and admin. I know what's ahead, I'm not anxiously scanning my list wondering what best to do next and I don't put off the less appealing jobs. My week has structure – like a proper job!

5. Capturing my processes

When it's only you, it's tempting to hold everything in your head, but that's not going to be helpful when the happy day comes that I need a virtual assistant because I'm heavily in demand! I'm an organised, logical thinker so I've capitalised on this strength. When I find myself sending the same email repeatedly, I save it as a template. I've mapped out client 'journeys' and automated things where possible to ensure it's professional for them and easy for me.

6. Networking

I joined networking groups to get known but it proved equally useful for practising talking about my business and discovering what questions this prompts. As a result, I changed how I describe what I do three times until I was comfortable with it. Meeting people energises me, and I can see some of these new acquaintances becoming friends already. Having positive people around makes such a difference. It also helps me develop ideas because I do my thinking by verbalising my thoughts, and the more I share with others, the more concrete and achievable those plans become for me.

7. Resolving the 'sales' thing

I know a lot of women struggle with the whole selling thing; it's like something icky you found in the fridge that you'd rather not deal with! Once I started noticing how I felt about sales interactions in everyday life, it got easier. For example, when I'm a buyer, I'm really uneasy if the offer isn't obvious because I'm worried there might be an embarrassing misunderstanding. This has convinced me to be clearer about how something might help someone and how much it costs. It's just information to help them make a decision.

8. Publishing my prices

I agonised like most people over pricing and finally followed Denise's advice to pick a price and go for it. I discovered – as she said would happen – that if you canvass people, they don't have a sense of the value of a product or service unless they need it. Despite hovering my finger over the publish button for at least half an hour, it made an instant difference to my confidence once my prices were up on my website. I'm transparent and it avoids wasting my and others' time if I'm not in their price bracket.

So, where am I now? I'm confident about what I offer, to whom and why. I have processes in place to make this easy and I'm investing in myself through learning and supervision. I'm working on building visibility, brand and reputation. I've got over my social media shyness and I'm getting encouraging responses to regular posts and blogs, which I really enjoy writing. My clients are finding me through word-of-mouth recommendation and I'm working hard to see that grow.I've learnt that when you fully commit to something, energy shifts, when you're at a low point is when breakthroughs happen, and above all, you can't wait for confidence. *Confidence and results come from consistent action.* That has become my daily mantra.

I wanted to use my story to show that just because you've been thinking about something for a long time, it doesn't mean it'll never happen. It's 10 years since that 'lifer' comment nudged my comfy existence but when the time was right and I fully committed, things started to happen. I also felt it important to be honest about the rollercoaster of emotions I experience and emphasise the importance of working on your mindset as much as your marketing! I say go for it and good luck!

BIO:

Celia Clark is a clarity coach who helps employed and self-employed women think clearly about their job so they can find happiness and success in their work. From unclear direction to work overload, confidence crises to promotion prospects, she helps clients simplify the complicated and lower the emotions so they can think clearly, see their choices and shape their future. She runs Inspires Coaching mostly online from her home in Oxford, UK, which she shares with her husband and two teenage sons. When she's not helping people grow, she's at the allotment persuading her flowers and vegetables to grow!

www.inspirescoaching.co.uk

10

ABOUT BLOODY TIME

Chrissy Church

Hi, I'm Chrissy of CC Therapy Winchester, and here is where it all began.

I was a 60s child, and as such, I grew up in a world that was techno free. I ate my breakfast, got my bike and the dog and off I went for the day, only coming home for essentials like food and if I was desperate for the loo.

Idyllic times when I look back, but occasionally there were problems. One summer I remember there was a group of kids, whose idea of fun was to beat me up every time I set foot out of the house (I was small for my age). I went to my dad, hoping he would shout at them or something, but he said 'you are the only one that can stop them, you have to stand up for yourself'. So, I did. I went straight out to where they were playing and headed for the biggest bully and promptly floored him with a head butt, the rest of them ran away.

I was so proud of myself, and when I turned around, I saw my dad, who was stood behind the fence, killing himself laughing. He later told me that I was only just tall enough to head butt the other child and was stood on tiptoe when I did it.

Being able to stand up for myself felt really good and I suppose it went to my head, because it soon became known around my friends, that if anyone was being bullied, then all they had to do was tell me and I would go and sort it, usually by a fist or a head butt.

Of course, as I got older, this behaviour stopped ... mostly ... but I was always acutely aware that there were people in the world who had no one to stand up for them.

Challenging the norms

In my early 20s I married a soldier (my lovely hubby of nearly 40 years) and was soon living in Germany. What a culture shock that was. Wives were seen as a nuisance, something to be barely tolerated, we were classed as 'excess baggage'. To begin with, I wouldn't say boo to a goose, but I really hated having to give my husband's last three numbers from his army number to identify myself to the medical professionals or if I bought any non-food items from the NAAFI.

The final straw for me was when I had to get my husband's permission to be sterilised after our second child was born. I started being more outspoken and stood up for myself and for my group of friends, all army wives. I had gained a reputation for not accepting behaviours and systems that had 'always been' and challenged the way the wives were treated. I knew that I had pushed the right buttons when I was asked to represent the Regimental wives at the very first Federation of Army Wives conference.

When I arrived at the conference, I was terrified. There were Brigadiers, Generals and other high-ranking officials, and the other representatives from the other regiments were mostly officer's wives. And there I was, a lowly Sergeant's wife. After all the introductions and the big-wigs had said their piece, the audience was asked if there were any questions, and I shot up out of my seat with my hand in the air, 'yes sir, I have some questions'. I'm not sure how long I stood up for, but I wasn't going to sit down until I had been able to put across numerous questions about how the lower ranks and their wives were treated, why weren't we treated as individuals and other questions I have long forgotten. The Federation of Army Wives successfully changed how wives were treated and still do even now.

My sense of fairness has accompanied me throughout my life, I hate injustice and I always follow up my feelings with practical actions.

Using my network for good

A friend's grandson was born with his organs outside his body and was very poorly for a long time. There was a certain type of over-the-counter medication which helped stop him from becoming constipated, which was very painful, but the manufacturer was discontinuing the product because it wasn't profitable, an explanation given to me by the general manager when I called them.

So, I lobbied the company, giving them written statements from my friend's family, GP and the surgeon who had performed most of the operations. I then contacted all of my friends, being an ex-army wife meant that they were all over the country, and asked them to go to every chemist in their area and purchase as much of this medication as they could, and again by using a network of friends, I arranged for these to be delivered to my friend in Scarborough.

At the end of the campaign, my friends had more than enough to keep them going for several months, but also, the manufacturer contacted me and had been persuaded by my campaign and the latest sales figures (ha ha), to continue manu-facturing the medication.

If I see that there is something fundamentally wrong which is negatively affecting someone, especially someone close to me, I have to find a way to change it and that is how CC Therapy Winchester came about.

Following my instincts

A dear friend's daughter, whom I am very close to, had suffered with her mental health for a very long time, and more so throughout her senior school years. Fortunately, most of the time we could talk about how she was feeling, and although I was always there for her I never felt as though I was making enough of a difference to her life because I simply didn't have the knowledge. Sometimes her mum would call me to tell me if she was having a particularly bad day and I would just 'happen' to pop in for a cuppa.

In her mid to late teens, her mental health deteriorated significantly, and she started to self-harm. Her school was able to refer her to a counsellor and although we didn't see much improvement to start with, her self-harming became less. I continued to support her and her mum the best way I could, by listening and asking questions.

Instinctively I knew never to ask 'why'? A question starting with *why* sounds accusing to me, and she has since asked me why I didn't ever ask her why she did or said certain things. My response was, 'if you wanted me to know why, I knew that you would tell me.' And the truth is, I never wanted her to feel as though I was judging her.

Filling a gap

Unfortunately, in 2016, when she reached the age of 18, it seemed that there was nowhere for her to go to get support. She was too old for CAMHS and not quite old enough for support in the community. Ever the practical person, I decided I was going to do something to plug that gap.

I researched several counselling courses and finally found one that I could do part time while I worked full time. My aim was to support those who fell between the gaps in the mental health services by becoming a counsellor. Mental health services were definitely lacking at this time; it was a very taboo subject and not many people admitted to suffering with mental health issues. Thank goodness things have improved since then, but there is still a long way to go.

I started the course in 2017. In the first year we were trained as hypnotherapists. I was sceptical at first, but as the course progressed, I was totally blown away. I began practising with friends and family as well as other course cohorts, and I was amazed at how effective it was and how quickly you could see results. The more I learnt, the more I realised that this is what I wanted to do. My tutor supported my decision to stop the 3-year course after the first year and told me that I was doing the right thing by sticking with the hypnotherapy; she was very complimentary and said that I was going to be a very good hypnotherapist.

When I told my best friend that I was going to specialise in hypnotherapy she said, 'about bloody time you realised that you are really good at this, you were born to do this.' Hence the title of my chapter 'About Bloody Time'.

CC Therapy Winchester is my practical way of helping and supporting people who are struggling with issues that are holding them back from living their best life possible.

· · ·

64

BIO:

Chrissy Church is 59, married, with two sons who are both married to wonderful ladies, and between them she has three gorgeous grandsons.

She started CC Therapy Winchester in August 2019, specialising in hypnotherapy to help work with anxiety, self-esteem and self-confidence to give people the sense of freedom that they deserve. Her ultimate goal is for her clients to step away from the baggage they carry around with them. It could be anxiety, stress or a fear or phobia, it can be anything that is preventing them from looking forward to the rest of their life with a sense of wonder and excitement.

www.cctherapywinchester.co.uk

11

LEARNING TO LOVE YOURSELF

Caitlyn Roberts

My brother and I were visiting my Grandparents in Malaysia. We had finished packing our cases to travel home and were weighing them to ensure they were within the weight limit. We both thought it would be fun to stand on the scales. Little did I know that this was the moment that would change my life. Aged 11 And weighing 11 stone, my unhealthy relationship with food and my body began.

This is the moment that stands out to me the most from my childhood. I remember always being aware that I was bigger than the other girls, but this was the first time I had seen the numbers on the scales. And even though I didn't really know what they meant, I remember knowing it was bad.

And so from this day I was self-conscious of my body and I disliked the way I looked. Fortunately I was lucky enough to be able to cover my insecurities with humour and a bubbly person-ality. If I was going to be the fat friend at least I would be funny and people would like me. Over the next few years I made friends with everyone. From the "cool" kids to the nerds and everywhere in between. And because of this I managed to survive secondary school without too much bullying. I still got comments from the odd boy here and there but in comparison to some I was pretty much left alone. Having two older brothers also helped I think.

I'll never forget the night that I was out with friends and one boy, not a particularly good friend but a friend nonetheless, looked at me and said, "Do you know, you would be the prettiest one out of all of your friends if only you lost weight". This comment has stayed with me and for a long time I believed it. I believed that only skinny girls could be pretty. I believed that if I lost weight I would be pretty. If I lost weight I would be accepted and boys would like me.

So fast forward to year 11 - the final school year. My prom was around the corner and I knew I wanted to lose weight and look the best I could. My dad and I joined a slimming club and from this I lost 3 stone. This club taught me that there were good foods and bad foods. It taught me that eating as much of the good foods as you liked was acceptable and other certain foods were off limits (like avocado).

My unhealthy relationship with food was magnified from this point onwards. Although I lost weight, I began to feel guilty anytime I ate something that was "bad food". The guilt then ate away at me. My dislike for myself grew stronger and stronger. I would self sabotage and binge.

Over the next 3 years I gained all the weight I had lost back, plus more. I then went on and tried every fad diet there was.

I tried; Shakes, meal replacements, the Egg diet, The cabbage diet, the intermittent fasting diet, the super unhealthy low calorie diet, and of course magic pills prescribed by the doctor that made your body reject any fat. You name it I have tried it. And it may not come as a shock to you but none of them worked. Oh don't get me wrong they worked for 10 days max, and then I couldn't sustain it and fell off the wagon which led to gaining all the weight back plus more!

Throughout this time I also found myself in a toxic relationship. At 19 I was pregnant and the biggest I had ever been. I was having to have extra tests because my BMI was so high. I had midwives telling me I needed to lose weight and to be healthy. For the first time I actually listened. This was the healthiest I had ever been. I was no longer doing it for myself but for my baby. I lost 10lbs during my first pregnancy. And considering my boy was 8lb 7 I think that's pretty good going.

After he was born I gained all the weight plus more back again. I told myself I didn't need to worry because I was planning on having another baby and so I would lose it then. I didn't like who I was and I used food for comfort. I barely went out unless it was for work or to see family, I stopped seeing friends and I hated the way I looked.

I then got pregnant with my daughter phoebe 2.5 years later. After experiencing a miscarriage she was a huge blessing. This time around my BMI was even higher and once again my pregnancy was classed as high risk. The labour was intense, and she got stuck and almost didn't make it. (That's a story for another day).

My baby girl was here, my family was complete. I had decided I didn't need to have any more babies, We had one of each and they were both perfect. This also meant I had no more excuses to stay fat. I started doing a few exercises at home and began to see my body changing slightly. Something in me clicked one night. The next day I joined the gym and never looked back.

I started off going to the gym 7 days a week by myself. First it was just on the cardio machines. Which I slowly increased each time. My eldest brother who had gone from a world champion powerlifter to a bodybuilder (over 100lbs lost) was my biggest inspiration. No way was I going to be the biggest one in my family now! He has helped me throughout my journey and still does to this day. There are no words that could ever thank him enough. I quickly realised that I needed to step things up a little, I hired a personal trainer and a nutritionist and within six months I was down 6 stone. I had more confidence, but I still did not like myself or the life I was leading. My relationship was the worst it had been. My fiancé was an addict and I could no longer support him as well as our children. I knew I needed to leave. I knew if I stayed I would continue to be in this unhealthy and unhappy cycle. Being miserable was no good to him, me or our babies. So we separated.

Now I know what you're all probably thinking, I must be the happiest I have ever been? Well you would be wrong. I was 24, the smallest I had ever been, out of a toxic relationship, getting lots of attention. And you're right I should have been the happiest I had ever been. But I wasn't!

This was the time that I realised I was still so unhappy. Losing weight was not the answer to everything. I still had a lot of work to do within myself and my self discovery. And slowly but surely I learnt to love myself. I learnt that my weight doesn't define me and that this process was a journey and was going to continue for years to come.

From this, one thing was super clear! I wanted to help others. I wanted to change people's lives. The way that my life had been changed. I wanted to be the person that helped others on their journeys too. Not just for the physical change but the emotional and mental change too. To me that was priceless.

So I set out on my new journey. I enrolled in a personal trainers course. I flew out to America to get my sports nutrition licence and I began helping other mums who were fed up and tired of not liking what they saw in the mirror. I set up boot camps and one-on-one sessions in their own homes.

Now I'm not going to lie, It has been a LONG and SLOW process. It's taken a while to get my name out there. And for people to know what it is that I am doing and offering. Also keep in mind at the time I was also working 40 hours a week with a 2 year old and a 4 year old as a single Mumma.

Slowly but surely I continued and the word got out. The hardest part for me has been battling my own insecurities.I knew that I still did not look like the other personal trainers that are out there. I dont have the perfect figure or defined abs on my stomach. But the more ladies I worked with, the more I realised that this was not what women wanted within a personal trainer.They wanted someone who knew what they were feeling, what they were experiencing and someone they could relate to. That was me. I can offer them that. I know what they are going through and the struggles that they are facing on the daily. I know this because I have been there and am still battling those same things. They trust me because of this.

So to start with I became anything and everything to my clients. I allowed them to contact me anytime of the day or night. I would respond, I would be there for them to support them no matter what. I would go to their houses to train them. I would do bootcamps in the park and I was charging very little. Have you heard of the saying, burning the candle at both ends? Yep that was the definition of what I was doing. I quickly realised that this had to stop. I had to set boundaries and create something that worked for me. And if I had one piece of advice for those looking at creating a business, that would be it. Create something that works for you!

Over the years that I have had my own business, I have invested so much into myself! I have learnt what my perfect client looks like and I have become more selective with who I chose to work with and my biggest take away has been that I can not help anyone who is not ready or willing to be helped. I know this because at one stage in my journey I was not ready to be helped. And there was nothing anyone could have done for me at this point. I no longer take it personally if a client cancels on me or pays for 10 sessions and only has one. This ultimately is their choice and I need to focus my time onto those who are ready. As hard and frustrating as this is, because I know how their life would change if they were committed.

So where am I at now I hear you ask? Well this in itself is a difficult question. We have had a global pandemic. And a lot has changed for me recently. I could no longer do in-person training which was what I loved to do. Therefore I have changed my focus to online clients. To help as many people as I can to live a healthier and happier life. We hone in on creating good habits that help aid mental and physical health. We look at the bigger picture, how we fuel our bodies, how we recover from workouts and how we listen to what our bodies need. This journey is way more than a weightloss journey. This is a journey to self discovery and to being healthy in Mind, Body and Soul.

BIO:

Caitlyn Roberts has dedicated her life to being the healthiest and happiest role model to her two children. As well as being on a mission to help others to love themselves.

www.facebook.com/caitlyn.roberts.336

12

HAVE BREAST PUMP – WILL TRAVEL!

Claire May

S eems a strange title for the start of an Event Management business, right? Read on – it was a pivotal moment!

I left school at 16 and started my career in a local travel agency via a YTS (younger readers may need to google) earning a massive £21 a week. A great opportunity to understand the logistics of travel, make people happy and see some of the world myself. Those were the days of flip charts for seating allocation, manual dial phones and nylon uniforms. A stint in London at a high-end travel agency opened my eyes to possibilities and I experienced my first business class flight to the United States. All very exciting stuff for a young girl.

However, my dream had always been to join the RAF. So, once I was an "adult" I completed the basic training and embarked on a different journey. At the start of the 90's and at the ripe old age of 24, I found myself in Germany moving troops left, right, and centre during Operation Desert Storm. Listening to the news as friends from our base went to war. A challenging yet exhilarating time, where I learnt so much about myself and acquired a singular skill set – being bossy with 200 young men seemed to come easily to me! I found myself at 3am on a Wednesday morning dealing with 18-year-old lads, covered in desert sand, who just simply wanted to get home to see their Mum and Dad.

Upon my return to the UK, it seemed a natural transition to combine the two skill sets I had acquired and so I moved into Event Management. A growing business sector full of promise and excitement. Over the years which followed, I travelled extensively, planning events, sourcing venues and hotels, investigating activities and finally escorting groups of high-networth individuals on some of the most amazing trips. This was the time of high spend, high reward, a pressure filled, astonishing time of top salespeople and high achievers. During this period, the high spots included single-handedly planning the conference logistics for 4000 guests on board a cruise ship. This incorporated simultaneous translation in eight different languages and I fully appreciate being lucky enough to work with adventurous clients; enjoying safaris in Kenya, diving at the Great Barrier Reef, champagne picnics at the foot of Christ the Redeemer in Rio and the slot machines of Vegas. Drama is never far away in any event, during my travels I dealt with some of the trickier situations. My heart still sinks when I think of my group of VIPS being fog bound in Agra and the subsequent transport delays due to funeral pyres, however, it also bursts with pride at the safe, but premature arrival of a little baby boy. I still like to think had he been a girl I may have had a name check!

A fabulous time, filled with wonderful opportunities, but fast forward 13 years and I found myself on a flight to Palma, hosting a 2000 delegate conference and leaving my 11-week-old daughter at home, with said breast pump in my hand luggage. It was at that point I realised I needed to take control of my life ….. but I didn't, like so many, I simply wasn't brave enough.

. . .

I spent the next few years in turmoil – juggling family life with
the expectations of my employer. Excuse after excuse followed,
my business partner needed me, my clients couldn't cope
without me, the staff had to have guidance, and the family
needed financial security. The long and short of it was, I didn't
have the balls to do what I would have told anyone in my position to do.

At some point in time and much to my horror, I realised that
I had spent the first few years of my daughter's life hiding
behind the most ridiculous excuses. For many months I travelled the globe with that blasted breast pump in my hand
luggage, driving the motorways of the UK and knowing every
bend and bump on the M1 during my regular commute to
Leeds. Finally, I hit rock bottom, exhaustion, a bout of pneu-
monia in Las Vegas, tears over a lost car at Gatwick Airport and
an economic downturn all gave me the push that I needed.

I took redundancy and left the comfort of a salaried job. I
then hid away, removed myself from anything work related and
cut all ties with industry colleagues. Opted out of trade communications, cancelled memberships and avoided calls from
anyone in my business sector; to this day I don't understand
why, but I think I felt a failure. Why hadn't I managed to maintain my career and family when so many people do, why had I
taken the easy route and opted for redundancy?

I'd created Amayzed at 2am on Tuesday morning, but the
name, website and logo just sat there. It was nothing more than
a "holding page". I didn't know what to do or how to start. It
was all just a bit too much. The easy option was to ignore it. I
became the perfect "school mum". I threw myself into primary
school duties – fundraising and school governance. Never
missing a permission slip deadline, making the most amazing
costumes, attending every assembly and listening to the most

awful musical renditions. Somewhere, along the way, I completely lost myself. Don't get me wrong – I loved being involved with the school and I was, obviously, pretty good at it. Completing grant applications, raising money, organising school events – it was all just second nature to me – but I wasn't me. Something was missing. I felt flat and hollow. A bit lost and alone.

Then, a phone call out of the blue from an old client who only wanted to work with me! Wow – the excitement, the buzz, a one-day meeting in London for 70 people. I could arrange and plan this with my eyes closed, but it was the boost I needed to get my mojo back. They really were a very small client, with one event a year, that's all it took. I felt my confidence return and slowly that one small client grew, and their one event became three, then regular monthly meetings and as they grew so did I.

As my self-belief returned, I found myself with another regular client and then another. All through word of mouth, all people who I had worked with before and all people who believed in me. A couple of free charity events soon got my name out in the local area and in 2015 I was invited to support a couple of festivals. Something out of my comfort zone and a steep learning curve but running a successful event for 18,000 visitors was just amazing, from a low to a high in six years.

There were stumbling blocks along the way, of course, the threat of action from my old employer filled me with doubt. Contacts in the trade had moved on and I had to start building relationships again. I even heard stories about me having had a "breakdown" which hurt at the time and knocked my confidence, although I can now laugh at them. Technology had moved forward in leaps and bounds, new processes in place, dealing with procurement officers, completing tender documents when previously a handshake would suffice. Returning to this new world, as a sole trader caused some issues, but with support and determination these were all overcome.

For many years I thought Amayzed should be delivering the high scale, corporate events of old. I questioned myself. Why was I not taking clients back to India or Dubai? Where was my target clientele? How could I grow and make money? But the world has changed and so have I. I know that I do not need to be an out and out salesperson, but that by offering the "me" factor and supporting my clients as they grow and develop, they in turn will do the same for me. Talking to other small businesses and attending networking events, made me realise that references and recommendations is by far the best way forward. This applies particularly in a sector where there is no tangible "purchase item".

My first client is still with me. I've seen changes in leadership and management, but they are still loyal to me and I to them. Delivering just one event a year for them now but I love the fact I recognise each attendee; I know the history of the speakers; I don't need them to tell me who is vegan or lactose intolerant. I know them and they know me. That's what is important.

Every event I deliver, whatever the size, whatever the venue, whatever country we are in – I take pride in. It's my name and my reputation on the line. That would be my advice to anyone, in any walk of life, take pride in what you do and deliver it to the best of your ability.

With the strange happenings of 2020 I found myself revaluating the business and without realising it, the direction of Amayzed Events had changed already. Many of my clients had already asked me to support them with additional services, such as membership management, website design and as a result Amayzed Business Support was born in the height of the pandemic. It may not be the heady days of airports and breast pumps but life is good and Amayzed rolls on – I work with a variety of clients now, all small independent businesses who use me as an extra member of their team.

The future for events is uncertain but Amazyed will be there, and will adapt to whatever is thrown at me.

As I typed this last sentence I took a phone call inviting me to join a team delivering an 850 sq m exhibition stand in Germany in 8 weeks' time – so let the madness commence.

BIO:

Claire is the driving force behind Amazyed Events & Business Support and has over 35 years' experience of organising group events. Claire supports businesses, associations and charities with all their event requirements, from venue sourcing, staffing, catering, pre- and post-event management and much more!

A lover of lists and spreadsheets, Claire is a highly organised and motivated individual. Her unique abilities and natural intuition enables her to react to, and resolve, any problems which may arise.

www.amayzed.co.uk

13

VELVET & ROSE...FOR WOMEN WHO LIKE A BIT OF STYLE AND GLAMOUR!

Shirley Leader

"**R**eally?" "What?" "Oh Wow!" "Why are you opening up a shop?"

These were some of the responses I received when I told friends and acquaintances that I was opening a womenswear boutique. Many were very supportive however, I was surprised by a few of the shocked looks that I received and it made me want to prove to them that I had made the right decision and that I was going to make it a success.

What made me start a business?

I spent most of my life after university in a corporate world. Science, brand equity, marketing, consumer insights, research and quality were the fundamental drivers of a successful product launch. These were drilled into me and in hindsight put me in good stead for starting a business especially in a consumer focused setting. What I was fundamentally missing in my repertoire was how to actually open up a shop and how to run it!

So how did I start this journey? I think that I was always meant to open up a shop. I remember 'playing shops' as a child, discussing opening a slipper shop with a university friend and then later a jewellery shop with a friend. Often, we don't act on these little ideas in the backs of our heads and we just follow the natural path which by coincidence or contacts or life changes is laid out for us. It is only when you are given the opportunity or chance to make a change in your life, that you start to consider building on that niggling idea. I left my corporate world as I no longer wanted to travel considerably to get to work, wanted to spend more time with my family and wanted more for myself plus I didn't want to work for anyone else. More importantly I wanted to act on that little idea of opening up a shop.

At this juxtaposition in my life, I had two key career moves a) to join the police force and b) open up a shop. Yes, you heard right, the police force! Again, that was something that I wanted to do since I was a teenager. I went to the 'meet and greet' and thought I really don't know if I can do this and I think it will be much harder than I envisaged. In parallel, I visited a Mum's Enterprise seminar in Angel, London and that cemented my decision in making that move! I picked up ideas from the talks, networked and felt empowered to make the move. I also enrolled on some courses run by my ex-corporate company in the fundamentals of how to start a business hoping to shorten the gaps in my knowledge.

Research is everything!

When you start your business, you are so excited by what you are going to embark on, that you forget to, or choose not to, do your homework properly. You think, "oh yes, it'll be okay". DO

YOUR HOMEWORK! Really look into your product. Is it the right product for where you are selling it, how much money do you have to spend on it and selling it? Where are you going to sell it? How are you going to sell it? Are you going online or bricks and mortar... etc, etc. Talking with other industry experts certainly helped me. I connected with another local shop through a friend and really picked their brains on everything I didn't know. That time was so valuable, and I'll always appreciate the time spent helping me. I visited many different towns and really wanted to stay local as again I wanted to reduce my travel time and be easily available for the days when I wasn't going to be at the shop. Plus, I wanted my local friends to shop there too! In the end I chose a town which had a good footfall and where many people visited. I was so pleased with this decision as footfall is everything for a new business.

Opening day

29th March 2018 was when I opened my boutique. I had a few lovely friends helping me set the shop up, my husband put the shop fittings in, but I contracted out the flooring and deco-rating, plus other key jobs. I was careful in not spending money loosely as I had a feeling that I would regret it if I did. The mayoress cut the ribbon and, joined by fellow friends and busi-ness owners, I opened my shop!

First Year

The first few months were a steep learning curve. I spent too much money on staffing and footfall was up and down. Some of the clothing was not quite right and I had bought too much...a common mistake. I quickly realised that I had to go online and by October I got some help to create a website and that helped me considerably but here again you are reliant on SEO and other areas which I am still trying to learn. I was pleased that I did this as Covid-19 was looming. Slowly, slowly footfall increased, and sales were going up.

Consumers

People buy from people. This is so true especially with independent businesses. How many times do you refuse to go into a shop if the owner hasn't treated you with respect and kindness? At Velvet & Rose we want everyone to feel that they are the most important person in the room. Even if the shop is full of people, we ensure that we acknowledge everyone. I know so much about my customers, their fears, celebrations, dress size, style etc and you just don't get that in a department store. Even when I am not in the boutique, I try to stay connected to them. It's important to me and them I believe!

So, what is running a business like?

It is challenging. Everyone has said that retail and the high street has changed so much over the years. With a fall in footfall, increased online activity, changes in the economy and consumer behaviour, you are sailing against a strong wind! You go to bed thinking about the business and wake up thinking of it. It is all consuming, just like a love affair! There are times where I wanted to just leave it all behind especially when you are not paying yourself, but something inside you gives you the strength to carry on. However, if it is not viable you have to draw a line under it. I love that you are your own boss and as all shop owners say, I love my customers. We are both embarking on a journey together!

Brexit, Covid, what next?

There are always challenges on the horizon whether you are

aware of them or not. You have everyday challenges such as a customer wanting to return an item, or a supplier you cannot get hold of, your card reader not working etc. Then you have the major ones such as Brexit and Covid-19. What the recent lockdowns have taught us is to be prepared for any interruption via your cashflow. Have money in the bank to bail you out. Constantly review your accounts and you should be okay – fingers crossed!

Networking

As a business owner you can feel pretty lonely at times. Friends and family who were there for you at the beginning become busy and/or lose interest and you are left to manage the daily burdens of your business. I found it invaluable to seek out other business owners whether in the same line of work or not. Some were just individuals but many were in Facebook groups or local area business groups. Some I took to straightaway and others I thought it is not for me. I think you know when an organisation is right for you and it is okay to walk away. Many organisations charge money due to the cost of running events and paying for marketing etc so do shop around as to what you are comfortable in paying for. The bottom line for me is that without networking I would not have started my business and would definitely have pulled out of it.

What would I do differently if I did this again?

Off the top of my head, I would buy less clothes at the onset, do more local research and pick a more central location. Not having a shop in the main thoroughfare means that you have to work that little bit harder to get people into your shop! It is manageable but you need to advertise more. I still have many people coming to the shop and saying "I have lived here for X number of years and I have not heard of your shop." Also, retail is so dynamic. No day is the same. You could get many sales one day and hardly any the next, so do be prepared for that. I had a well-paid job with a regular wage and moving away from this can be very challenging. So don't expect a bed of roses straightaway!

The future

I hope to build on my success. When I openly questioned my success in the past, someone said to me "you are a success". That stuck with me. I couldn't see it at the time but now I believe it is true. Running your own business in today's climate is truly challenging. Why do we do it? I did it to prove to myself that I could do it, to show my children that anything is possible and to make a difference to my customers. I love fashion but even more so I love to see other women (and men) love fashion too and to feel better about themselves.Anything can happen in the future. I need to be agile and expect the unexpected. Once I stop enjoying what I am doing I would then stop and move on. Retail is changing every day. We just don't know how we will be selling in 10 years' time or even 5? Online is so predominant right now but social media selling is on the rise and, what portals for selling will be available to us in the future? All we can do is adapt and to enjoy every day, good or bad!

So to anyone reading this, I wish the best success and if you ever need a chat, do look me up!

BIO:

Shirley Leader is the owner of Velvet & Rose, womenswear boutique in Petersfield, Hampshire. She opened her boutique in March 2018 after spending more than 23 years working at a Research and Development company. Through researching, learning, networking and support from friends and family she finally realised her dream of running a shop. Shirley is a strong believer in that if you work hard enough you can achieve your goals. She loves selling beautiful clothes; great clothing, all at affordable prices and enjoys building relationships with her customers! "We are both embarking on a journey together!"

www.velvetandrose.co.uk

14

A DREAM THAT YOU WISH...

Kate Robbins

I'm not sure I'll ever feel comfortable calling myself a businesswoman. Even though my company has been established for a year and a half, that term still triggers imposter syndrome for me. Who am I to be running a business? What gives me the right?! If it were anyone else, that would be exactly the word I'd choose, but for some reason when it comes to me - it doesn't feel right. I'm still learning to challenge my inner saboteur but if I allowed her to dictate everything I do, I wouldn't have started my company at all. I have no business training or experience, just a collection of skills and a passion for what I do. It has been a big learning curve and I have faced so many challenges on my business journey so far, but I can say with my whole heart that it has been one of the most rewarding experiences of my life, and I'm so grateful to be where I am today.

Rewind a year and a half, my professional career had been a bit all over the place – I'd had more jobs before 30 than most people had had in their entire lives. I've worked in various industries and have been fortunate enough to work some fun and exciting jobs. Cabin Crew for Virgin Atlantic, an Airside Operations Controller (you know, the people at airports with the table tennis bats!) and even a Princess at Disneyland, just to name a few. But no matter what job it was, no matter how much I believed - this is it, I've found my calling - nothing ever stuck. This wasn't for lack of trying; I always do everything at maximum capacity, throwing myself wholly into everything I do, but for some reason - they all ended the same way. With me losing motivation and burning myself out by forcing myself to continue until breaking point. I suppose in my heart I've always known that being an entrepreneur was my path to happiness, but I've struggled so much with self-doubt that I've always held myself back, putting barriers up before even starting.

I'm a very creative person, and this is reflected in my many hobbies. These were things I always loved spending my time doing, but never believed anyone would actually pay me for – that's why it's called a hobby! My Nana taught me to sew when I was a teenager. I developed a love of designing and creating costumes and elaborate outfits, something I still hold the same value for to this day. There's something about seeing a pile of fabric turn into something beautiful that just feels so satisfying. But that's just something I like to do in down time; it never felt like a skill. For as long as I can remember, I've always loved to dance, sing, act and perform, and I'm almost always rehearsing a play or musical – but that's also just for fun. There's no WAY I would ever have a chance of earning a living with it, I'm nowhere near good enough. Right?

Wrong. I was forced to reassess these beliefs when I was successful in an audition for Disneyland Paris in November 2014 and invited out to work there on a permanent contract to play Elsa, Mary Poppins, and several of their furry friends - a real performing job at the most magical place on earth! Somebody pinch me, this can't actually be real - but it was. I really did have the time of my life working out there, dancing down Main Street on the parades, meeting thousands of families in meet and greets, and even being cast in the Frozen Singalong Show to perform six shows a day. But yet again, even though this was my dream job, I somehow still managed to burn myself out and had to return home after just one year. Working at Disneyland as a Character Performer meant so much to me, not only because it was truly a dream job, but also because of my sister, Rowena.

Rowena and I had such a strong bond as sisters and did everything together – our mother even insisted on dressing us in matching outfits whenever she could! There were only two and half years between us and despite being the older sibling, I often ended up doing her bidding and taking the blame for any trouble we got into.

When she was 2, Rowena was diagnosed with a brain tumour and given less than a year to live. She defied the odds and for her fourth birthday, the Make-A-Wish Foundation granted her wish to go to Disneyland Paris. I have the most treasured memories from that trip which I'll hold in my heart forever. On that holiday, for that short while, she was no longer the terminally ill child; in pain, subjected to tests, operations, radiotherapy, and pity. She was just a little girl, free to enjoy herself in the most magical place on earth. She passed away just four months later. In my time as a Character Performer at Disneyland, I felt honoured and privileged to have the opportunity to give to others the gift that had been given to me, 17 years earlier.

I didn't realise it until many years later, but the trauma of the loss of my sister when I was 7, and then my father when I was 14, took its toll on my mental health and I was diagnosed with borderline personality disorder when I was 22. BPD is a condition usually born out of traumatic childhood experiences which manifests in extremely intense emotions, mood swings, chronic fear of abandonment, feelings of worthlessness and suicidal tendencies. I struggled with feelings of despair for many years after I returned from Disneyland, unable to work due to my poor mental health and hopeless at the prospect of any kind of future. I felt trapped – unable to hold down an employed position and too unskilled and useless to attempt entrepreneurship. I received several different forms of therapy and through a lot of hard work and the unconditional love and support of my partner, friends, and family, eventually started to feel little glimpses of hope for the future. I still couldn't imagine running my own business and attempted both employment and education again - but even with the knowledge of my mental health issues, I still faced the same struggles with burning out, and didn't know why. I was in a much healthier place and really wanted these jobs to work – so why did I find it so difficult?

I did some serious self-assessment and realised that the job I enjoyed the most by far, was performing at Disneyland, so I decided to seek out as close a job as I could that wouldn't require me living abroad. I was aware of princess party companies but didn't have the confidence in myself to start my own company, so I began working for a company based about an hour away from me, performing as various characters at children's parties and events. I thoroughly enjoyed every single booking I did but the distance I had to travel for each booking wasn't ideal. After 10 months, I finally built up the confidence to take the plunge.

In August 2019, I started making plans to launch my own children's character entertainment company. I gathered a small team of four people I knew from various performing jobs I'd had, and we volunteered at a few charity events that year to build interest. We received very positive feedback from the charity events we did and began getting enquiries before I even had a name for the company! In January 2020, Imaginacts Entertainment Ltd was born and officially launched. I knew absolutely nothing about running a business and had no idea whether I'd be successful or not - all I knew was that I had a collection of skills and that I had to try. Before I knew it, the diary began getting fuller and fuller each month - and then came the 23rd March 2020 - lockdown. I was devastated. How on earth could such a young company providing in-person events entertainment survive this?

Sometimes ideas strike us when we least expect it, which I feel is part of the beauty of running your own business - you find you have the motivation to act on these ideas when they hit, even if it's just scribbling a few notes down to build upon later. I realised that I was actually in a position to help families with young children by giving them something to look forward to during the lockdown. I began offering character video calls on a free or pay-what-you-feel basis and was absolutely overwhelmed by the support and generosity not only of clients, but also my performers who volunteered their time with no guarantee of payment. I learnt that I had a lot more resilience and strength than I had even realised. Somehow, I – someone with zero business training or experience – was able to adapt and overcome the challenges presented by the pandemic. It was stressful and very hard work, but somehow, contrary to my experience of employed work, I always managed to find the motivation to face the challenges head on and work out a solution.

As I'm writing this in August 2021, Imaginacts now has 16 characters with more on the way, 10 performers, and over 70 glowing reviews. I am now one half of the directorial team, having asked one of my performers and very close friend, Fi, to join me as a co-director; knowing when to ask for help is a necessary skill in business. Her skillset complements mine perfectly and without her, Imaginacts wouldn't have grown half as much, or half as quickly. We have bookings every weekend, and always have at least five ideas in the pipeline for the future. Business meetings are fun, and we genuinely look forward to our work days. Three years ago, I felt totally hopeless and was truly ready to give up on life – I would never have believed you if you'd told me I'd be where I am today. I feel so deeply grateful to have had the support and encouragement from my friends and family to begin this adventure.

I once read a brilliant piece of advice about swapping imposter syndrome for brilliant conman syndrome – try swapping your thoughts of 'I don't know how to run a business – I should just quit now!' for 'Do I know how to run a business? Absolutely not! Does anyone else know that? Nope, mwahaha!'. I've found that makes the challenges seem a little bit more manageable. My advice to anyone considering starting their own business is that if you have that itch, it won't ever go away until you give it a try. If you have skills that can be put to good use, don't brush them aside as nothing more than hobbies. And if you've never found a job that felt completely, perfectly right - create your own. So, what are you waiting for?

BIO:

Kate Robbins co-owns Imaginacts Entertainment Ltd, a children's character entertainment company based in Hampshire. Their mission is to create authentic character experiences to make little dreams come true. Kate has always found the magic of fairy tales inspiring and comforting in times of need and loves to share that magic with every child she meets. Through custom made costumes, highly trained and experienced performers, and a passion for making magical memories to last a lifetime, Kate and the Imaginacts team bring beloved children's characters to life – even you might believe you've met the real deal!

www.imaginacts.co.uk

15

STRESSED TO DRESSED

Victoria Hamilton

I t was January 1st 2016 and I was sat in tears at my parent's house after a fabulous evening the night before celebrating both New Year's Eve and our friends' first wedding anniversary. It was a wonderful evening, full of love, laughter, fizz and gin, but it went from glam to grim in just a few hours.

I woke up the next morning with a huge cloud over me. I felt sad and my mind was heavy. Reality hit, the New Year had begun, and I was due to return to work in a few days as my second round of maternity leave was coming to an end.

I was lying in bed and my dad came in for a chat when he casually asked me about going back to work. I completely broke down and was in floods of tears. The tears had obviously been building for some time, but why? What was wrong with me? I loved my job before I went on maternity leave, I loved my industry before I went on maternity leave, and I had poured my life and soul into studying and qualifying for my CIPD in my HR profession. But this time returning to work was entirely different, something just felt off.

The reality dawned. I had another little girl who I very much wanted more time with, not less, plus the mum guilt started to build. I didn't want to miss out on all the firsts as my eldest daughter navigated her way through the first few months of primary school. This played on my mind constantly. Was I doing the right thing working? I needed to find a life-work balance, not a work-life balance. It was these thoughts that began to eat away at me. I just couldn't shake this feeling off, in my gut I knew I was doing the wrong thing, but I carried on. This is life, this is what we have to do.

The first few months back at work were okay, not terrible, not great, just okay. The gradual pull, however, of balancing everything kept pulling me down. I knew I was starting to lose myself, but I wasn't truly aware of how much I was losing myself at the time.

Something had to give

Fast forward 10 months to October 2016 and I had really lost my way. Both physically and mentally, I didn't feel happy, I was stretched too far with work and home and as a consequence my health was suffering. I lost my confidence, self-esteem and style. I wasn't giving anyone the full attention they needed, including myself. I cancelled seeing friends, I struggled to get up some days and I was tired all the time. I was dressing in anything that felt easy as opposed to stylish and my self-care routine was non-existent. I didn't feel like me at all.

I visited my GP; they did various tests and signed me off work. I felt relieved.

The day I got my blood results back I had taken my daughters to spend half term with my parents caravanning. You can imagine how excited two little girls were at that prospect! While there I got a call from my GP to say that my bloods were back, and my thyroid levels were all over the place and would need further tests. I was also told it was likely I had an autoimmune disease called Hashimoto's. Basically, in short, this is where your immune system attacks itself from the inside. It made sense. After reading up on the symptoms, I was shocked at how many I could tick off the list. I booked in to see my GP that week to discuss everything in more detail, but a weight was suddenly lifted, and I felt a sense of clarity and peace that I hadn't felt in sometime.

Why don't you just leave?

As I was with my parents I talked them through the call with my GP. My dad quite matter-of-factly asked: 'why don't you just leave (your job)?' He was right, why didn't I? I was unhappy. I had fallen out of love with what I did, and I was really struggling mentally with the day-to-day tasks that were required of me. I hated that I felt like I was letting people down that I both worked with and highly respected.

There's a lot that happened between that light bulb moment and me actually leaving my HR role, but I did it, it happened. With the loving support of my husband, I actually resigned and was unemployed.

What now?

Do you believe in destiny?

A friend of mine shared on her socials that she was training to qualify as a personal stylist. I was instantly intrigued and messaged her; she sent me the details and within minutes, with the encouragement of my family, my biggest cheerleaders, I had booked the course for myself! I think at the time I wanted it more as a personal benefit so I could regain my own personal style and confidence, but as soon as I arrived at The Fashion Lounge in Westfield London on a bright February day something just clicked and I knew instantly I was going to go all in on making this my career.

I felt it in my soul. Destiny.

Before losing my way I was a confident woman, I was career driven, took pride in my appearance and loved everything that life offered. If I could lose my identity, style and confidence surely lots of women were feeling this way too? That's when I knew that this career was the one for me, I wanted all women to feel fabulous, empowered and ultimately wanted to teach women how to go from stressed to dressed.

That was February 2017 and on April 1st 2017 Victoria Hamilton Lifestyle was launched and out there in the world.

Stressed to dressed

Having experienced this first-hand, I want every woman to know that she can be confident and stylish, whatever those terms mean to her.

Style is extremely personal, and when working with a client I take into consideration more factors than you may realise, including lifestyle, personality, and budget.

A perception of great style is that a higher end budget means you can be more stylish: this is not the case. Local boutiques, the high street and online retailers all offer a wealth of stylish pieces to suit all budgets. The key is knowing where to look. Luckily for my clients, I do!

I offer clients a range of personal styling experiences including colour analysis, showing women what colours and tones suit them; wardrobe edits; and personal shopping. I love every second I spend working with my clients, showing them the magic of my style secrets and how to enhance their already fabulous selves.

From launching my business, I've always struggled with the job title of "Personal Stylist" I find it can be perceived as pretentious or elitist; I'm much more your 'stylist next door' type of girl, which led me to positioning and titling myself as a 'Style and Confidence Cheerleader'. After all, that's what my clients need – not only someone who understands their style and confidence struggles, but someone who can expertly and gently guide them by building their style and confidence levels, striking the perfect balance between expert and cheerleader.

I've styled clients for media events including royal events at Buckingham Palace and royal charities. My work has been featured in both print and online mainstream media including being interviewed by BBC Radio. I've been invited to London Fashion Week, Manchester Fashion Week, Winchester Fashion Week and even attended a show at Paris Fashion Week – that trip was a real pinch me moment.

Well-known and established high street brands and online retailers have collaborated with me to style clients for press and PR events, as well as for hosting in store style workshops and fashion shows. One highlight was presenting a style talk for Hampshire, IOW and Thames Valley Police force on International Women's Day.

I've been privileged to style a whole range of women, seeing transformations happen right before my eyes in a matter of minutes and others over a period of time. Some of these women wanted to style with me for fun, or had lost their confidence after having a baby, after a health scare or a change to their family dynamic. Each client is unique in their styling needs and I appreciate every single one.

What I do is a privilege, women trust me with their fears and what's happening in their lives, quite often sharing insecurities they don't feel confident enough to share with their friends and family. What I do is more than just dressing women; I really feel it's my calling, and I truly love it. I feel alive.

· · ·

The future's bright, the future's stylish

Running your own business can be quite lonely and challenging at times, especially if your background was in the corporate world, or a world full of people. A lot of the time it's just you. One of the best and most rewarding things I ever did to counteract that was joining local networking groups where I met like-minded entrepreneurs, all striving to make a difference in the world.

Through networking and running my own business, I've learnt so much about the 'how' and technical aspects of managing my own business – this was the biggest learning curve for sure! While I knew I wanted to style women and build their self-confidence, what I didn't really understand is that I would also have to be the social media consultant, marketing manager, photographer and accountant for my business, too. Having a great network of entrepreneurs around me meant there was and continues to be a cheerleader for all of those areas championing me on with advice to help me succeed.

Being the CEO of your own business means you are always looking for new ways to enhance your business and service offerings. I've added various trainings and qualifications to my styling business over the years, and I am also training to offer my style experiences as a licensed and accredited Style Coach™. There is a subtle difference between the two, with my style experiences now including work on mindset, emotions, body confidence and a little NLP rather than just pure personal styling and personal shopping.

It's so much more than that.

Style Coaching™ is more than the clothes you wear or buy: it's a self discovery of who you are, who you want to become and what barriers are in your way, or what help you need to overcome certain triggers. I help women to become their true, most fabulous, stylish self.

I'm truly excited for the future of Victoria Hamilton Lifestyle and I cannot wait to take you on your own style discovery and teach you how to go from stressed to dressed!

BIO:

Victoria is a Style Coach™ and Confidence Cheerleader. As a value-driven wardrobe specialist and cheerleader of self-acceptance, she seeks to empower women going through the many transitional stages of their lives with the tools they need to feel confident and happy within themselves through the clothes they wear. Victoria uses a combination of technical styling, gentle support and confidence coaching with expert advice, encouragement, and positivity along the way.

Victoria is like the girl next door with a long list of magical styling secrets you can apply to the clothes you already own, allowing you to regain control of your wardrobe and style, taking you from stressed to dressed.

www.victoriahamiltonlifestyle.co.uk

16

AND THERE I HAD IT, THE TITLE I
HAD BEEN SEARCHING FOR...

Charlotte Lester

It was the end of winter in 2013, I was in my corporate JOB working as an Executive Assistant when I found out I was expecting my first child. Excited, nervous, scared – I had all the feels! Fast forward a year and it was time to make a huge decision, do I go back to work or be a stay at home mum? You see I thought back then those were my only options. I felt stuck, being on maternity leave was amazing, spending time with my new born baby. However it also left me feeling lost. I had lost my confidence, I had lost my identity and therefore, I knew being a stay at home mum was not the right choice for me and for my daughter. Afterall, she deserved me at my best, and I was most definitely not at my best!

The decision was made, I was going back to my JOB. So, off I went preparing for my return to work, childcare, work times, routines, everything was organised. That day approached so fast, my first day back. While commencing my morning two to two-and-a-half hour commute I was left with so many mixed emotions, was I doing the right thing? How was I going to fit in full-time work and still be a great mum? How would I keep my mental health in check? I had no idea how or if this was going to work, but I was going to give it my best try. I had agreed to my work hours which consisted of leaving the house at 5:30am every morning to arrive at work at 7:30am and start my day in order for me to leave the office at 4pm each day to get home at 6:30pm and collect my daughter from nursery in time – except from Fridays, where I worked from home and my daughter had a later start of 9am until 4pm.

The first day back saw me sobbing on the phone to my (now) husband, after my computer/equipment was not ready for my return, and my laptop was not ready and therefore, I had to come into the office on the first Friday back which sent me into a spin trying to work out nursery drop off and pick up because I would not make it there in time for my daughters Friday nursery hours. Then wham, in comes the mum guilt.

After 6 months back I got promoted, which was much needed and a huge fresh start for my work life! But continuing with the long commute, the daily juggle of motherhood, life and work saw me on a never ending hamster wheel. After a couple of years we decided to have our second child, this time I knew things would need to change drastically. Not only were we adding another human being to our lives, but our eldest was due to start school, and there was no way I could continue with my current job and commute and get back for school pick up. After much discussion between my husband and I, we decided that I would step away from my current JOB and look for something else that was going to work around our life – not the other way around! Financially my husband could earn more money being self-employed, for me, I could only earn my salary and never got overtime even when I worked more hours.

There I was, sat 'Googling' work from home jobs. And it was there that I found out about virtual assistants. I thought, I can do that. Off I went, working out the tools, tech and strategies required. I purchased a course to become a virtual assistant and after a couple of months I had my first client. That was it. That was the time I truly believed I could do this! I never thought little-old-me could run a business, I always thought in order to make money, I had to work hard for someone else in a JOB. After having my second daughter, I continued working as a virtual assistant but I started feeling bored and frustrated. I had taken a step back in my career and did not feel a challenge anymore. I am someone who needs a challenge, so off I went to trusted 'Google' again to work out what my work title actually was. I was doing more than within the remit of a virtual assistant, but I was not charging more – in fact I was charging less! And there I had it, the title I had been searching for...On-line Business Manager (OBM). I purchased a book about being an OBM just to make sure that was definitely the route I was going to take. And that was it. I started to market as an online business manager, started telling my clients that I was following the OBM path and most of them wanted to be on the journey with me which was such an amazing feeling. Then it happened, I was working all the hours, from 5–6am through to midnight, I was exhausted, drained and feeling miserable. This was defi-nitely not why I started my business. So I reconnected to my vision, my why and my current business model and I realised it was not aligned. I was way over capacity, and felt as if I was not providing the level of service my clients deserved, so I took the jump...The jump I had been putting off for a long time, I took on sub contractors to help. And after just a couple of months I realised everything was aligning in business and life. My role in business was actually the leader. Before I knew it I was leading my very own business support agency. Year on year we were doubling our revenue and growing rapidly.

I also realised that my mission was to serve as many female business owners as possible to scale their business without burning out. Mental health is the heart of everything I do and stand for, not just in business but life, so it made sense to include that in my mission. However, with the agency overheads, it was not going to be a low cost offering, and only established business owners would be able to invest in their business on the agency level, so what about the other amazing business owners out there that needed our support?

Over the past year the business has grown massively not just in revenue, and team but in offerings and expertise too. As of today, the business has 10 active team members, including a fabulous account manager supporting us and our clients/team. I focus on the strategy side, providing advice and guidance on growing your team, leveraging your time and automating in order to gain more time and money back! We also have a group programme aimed at helping business owners to incorporate systems into their business to get themselves out of the overwhelm weeds. Along with other mini courses, and our brand new products range! Wow, we have been busy bees!

Could I have ever imagined I would be leading an 'adult' business 10 years ago? Absolutely not! But I am, and of course, there have been many, MANY ups and downs, I would not change it for the world. If you are feeling like you are stuck in a job, that you have no choice but to work hard for someone else, that you would never be able to run a business because that is for other people. I want to tell you, that is not true at all, I had the same thoughts, and had I not pushed through those thoughts, I probably would still be thinking the same. Life is too short to not enjoy every moment.

BIO:

Charlotte is the founder of Simple Operations to Scale™ (SOS), Simple Systems to Scale™ (SSS) and the Burnout Slayer™ Toolbox. Also CEO of CVA Associates, a digital consulting company that specialises in scaling businesses through simple operations and systems while avoiding burnout.

Charlotte learnt how difficult it was for small businesses with limited resources to grow their business.

www.cva-associates.com

17

FREE TO BE SAFE, SAFE TO BE FREE

Hayley Thomas

Being free to be safe and safe to be free is how I desire to live my life, and by being in control of my destiny as a businesswoman, it is absolutely true, for the most part!

You will, however, most definitely be forgiven for wondering how these two emotional states can coexist! Recently, I worked with a good friend of mine who is an amazing business coach. When talking about these desired feelings, she mentioned how contrary freedom and safety can sound. It is true: freedom makes you think of no ties, wind in your hair, the ability to go with the flow. Being free comes with risk and an added spice of potential danger, right?? Safety feels more closed in a way, more structured, more sedate even; it means being protected and secure with a degree of certainty, right?? Well, it all seems to come down to your personal definitions and what these concepts really mean to you.

To me, the balance of these seemingly contradictory drivers is what life is all about! I shall try to explain, so stay with me!

. . .

Freedom then and now

So, freedom. My interpretation of what freedom means to me has evolved and adapted countless times over the years. A lot of moons ago (think late teens and in my twenties), freedom meant no ties to keep me from any last-minute travel plans or crazy adventures. And those who know me well, know I rode that freedom all over the world as I explored various continents and cultures, as well as crazy heights, with only a bungee rope or a parachute to slow me down. In order to finance my shenanigans, I was employed full time, when not studying. That employment was very much a means to an end, rather than a way of life or pursuit of a lifelong career. The safety aspect of my life then came from having a solid family home base that I knew, no matter what happened, I could always return to.

Some would maybe see this as frivolous or escapist or even immature!! Not planning for the longer term and living as though life needs no commitment to more grown up things. In some ways I agree, now sat here in my late 30's with arguably fewer concrete or material "achievements" in my life than a lot of my friends and peers. But (and it is a big but) I regret nothing! The memories and experiences I collected through my younger years have stayed with me and gone a long way to shaping who I am as a person.

Where I am in my life now, freedom has changed to something a little subtler than the far-flung trips and crazy things. (Though I still absolutely love to travel and can't wait to get back out there again after the craziness of the pandemic!) One of the massive joys of self-employment is being master of my own timetable. We arrange our family schedule on our terms, and as my husband is also self-employed and our son is home educated, we have massive flexibility and freedom for our activities. The space to be present in each other's day is the main focus of our lives and to experience life together is a blessing. I firmly believe life is for living now, not one day, and that waiting for a set of imagined expectations to be achieved before allowing ourselves to truly experience love and life is the exact opposite of what being free means.

As I have evolved through my life from solo adventurer to wife and mother, the challenges of life have come in thick and fast, especially over the last 10 years. But my desire to live my life in freedom, as defined by me and those closest to me, has remained at the forefront of why I do what I do.

Safety

As I have hopefully managed to explain, I am a person who thrives on freedom and the need to see new things and meet new people, but in absolute contrast to that, I am really resistant to change. And here steps in the longing to feel safe. I like change on my terms, to my directions. Unexpected, sudden change can often send me reeling. Even if I know it is for the better and will be painless, I balk at the idea of things being different.

Safety means I am strong and held by myself and those I choose to keep close around me so I can be who I am and give the best of me. This is not an easy feat to accomplish; it takes daily work and practice to develop faith in ourselves that doesn't wobble at the whim of others. Keeping closest to us those who believe in us and light us up is extremely important but paramount is developing our ability to stand in our own power and feel safe there, as we are. As my business has developed over the years, a strong spiritual practice has become integral to not only my offering to my clients, but to me and my daily rituals. When I follow what I know is my best practice (trust me this isn't all the time, we are all only human!) my heart feels full of joy and potential; I am safe and free to be me.

Another big aspect of feeling safe and secure is the financial element. As I mentioned, different choices in my younger years saw me spending my disposable income on experiences and memories as opposed to material things like houses!! Being able to live comfortably without stress and worry and provide for my family is the safety I mean here.

This looks different for each individual and family and I believe no one is right or wrong in how they wish to experience this. I am lucky to have a beautiful home that we rent, over-looking a stunning view of fields and woodland. We have amazing friends next door who have been an incredible support through the lockdowns and beyond. I work from home and am free to switch between work and home mode at a moment's notice. Safety shows itself in mysterious ways.

My path to self-employment

The safety of employment has always been rather seductive to me, guaranteeing a wage on the certain day of the month, paid holiday etc. So, how did I get to be self-employed in the first place you wonder? Well, I shall tell you, briefly.

Some time back in the early 2000's, I came back from university with a history degree. I moved back in with my folks, which was quite the culture shock, and had six months of working in my previous seasonal fun jobs. The realisation that I had to get a proper grown up job came crashing in, and I started working at HSBC in their mortgages department.

A far cry from anything to do with my degree, as well as being miles from where I had imagined I would be in life at this point, but that would be another story. Five years went by in a flash, on a decent wage and with great colleagues and many trips to far-flung places. Then things came to a bit of an abrupt halt. With the financial crash in 2008/9, we were told in November 2009 that almost 300 of us would be being made redundant. I remember that day vividly; many people were crying, others were cross and rather a lot of us went to the pub that lunchtime and didn't return to work until the next morning!

Personally, it was a major turning point in my life. The initial shock of realising I was losing my job was quickly replaced with the epiphany of an opportunity. This job wasn't what I wanted for the rest of my life, but like many people I know, staying on the path of least resistance and security was an easy honey trap. I had to do some soul searching and really think about where I wanted to go from there. I knew that I had always yearned after the idea of the freedom of being self-employed and not having to listen to a boss, but the security of employment was a big thing to give up. I believe you are afforded only a handful of these big pivotal moments in life to truly change where you're headed in one big fell swoop, so I grabbed it with both hands!

I began with a year-long qualification in Sports and Remedial Massage, and it was the beginning of an incredible journey. I couldn't have imagined all those years ago where I was going to be ten years later, still offering the sports massage that I love, but also growing as a person and a business to become an Energy Practitioner and Spiritual Teacher. My business offering has expanded over time, in the same ways as I have I guess, energetically, spiritually, and indeed financially.

Growing through change

A lot of the changes I have been through in my business have been as a result of life events out of my control, and during the last decade I've had more than my fair share really! This is not a fact I lament; I am a firm believer that everything in life has a lesson attached, but I will admit there have been times that I have doubted my ability to carry on.

I have lost close relatives and friends, both to death and disconnection, moved house umpteen times (a chore I utterly despise with my whole resistance to change thing!), had four surgeries for various ailments, and experienced more physical and emotional pain than I ever thought possible. To go into all that would take far more pages than I have here to be honest, but it isn't all doom and gloom!

I also found my husband and soul mate and had our son who is the absolute light of my life. My boys are with me and behind me in everything I do. I know I am strong on my own, but with them I feel anything is possible. Knowing I am held in a loving family dynamic allows me the safety that I crave, and the way we have arranged our lifestyle means I am also able to live freely. The two go hand in hand for me. The most recent challenge, as it has been for so many, has been the pandemic. Each lockdown and measure put in place has caused me to question whether I can keep going more in these last 18 months than ever before. But I have kept on keeping on; I think I am too stubborn not to! I am eternally grateful that I have been able to come back each time, not just surviving but growing and becoming stronger in my business and in myself.

So, there you have it. The story, in brief, of how I came to be a business woman all those years ago. It has been one hell of a ride so far, but I am incredibly lucky and grateful. I hope my story shows that whatever it is that lights you up or fills your heart with joy is possible.

I am free.
I am safe.
I am strong.
I am loved.
Life is incredible.

BIO:

Hayley Thomas is a Spiritual Teacher, Energy Practitioner and Sports and Remedial Massage Therapist based in Romsey, Hampshire. She has a holistic approach to supporting her clients and works to move them out of pain, whether that pain is physical, emotional, or spiritual, and helps them to restore balance. Hayley enjoys making the "hippy dippy" world she adores accessible for everyone, from those looking to expand their existing spiritual practice, to those with a calling in life for something they can't quite put their finger on, yet!

www.miaza.co.uk

18

ME VERSUS THE MIND MONKEYS

Laura Porter

I never set out to have my own business although looking back on my life I think I have always been fiercely independent, happy in my own company and confident that I could make my way in the world without relying on anyone else. As a child my unflinching response to that time honoured question "What do you want to be when you grow up" was always "I'm going to be an artist" I smile to myself that this isn't so very far from my current place.

My name is Laura and I run my own eponymous interior design consultancy "Laura Porter Interior Design". This year the business reaches it's 11-year anniversary and fortunately for me, it has been my most successful year yet. However, like many of the beautiful souls contributing to this book it has been a long and winding road with highs and lows and there have been too many times when I have collapsed in a ball sobbing "I just can't do this anymore" This is my story....

The earliest seedlings of my design career began aged 18 on a one-year Art and Design Foundation course. This year opened me up to all the possibilities that I had been longing to test out in this broad sphere and I realised it was no longer acceptable to keep saying "I'm going to be an artist" It was time to nail my colour to the mast, to get specific and define the nuances of creating that I enjoyed the most. Good tutors steered me down the path of 3D design and somehow, before I knew it, I was celebrating achieving a place at Nottingham Trent University to study Interior Architecture and Design.

I spent four incredibly hard years working in the university studio from 9–5 everyday learning all aspects of the trade from colour theory, history of architecture, practical building techniques and vocabulary as well as CAD design. At the time I found it terrifying and already the mind monkeys were playing havoc with me *"You're too stupid to understand all of this, you will never ACTUALLY get a job doing this, why don't you give this up?"* I stuck at it and gave it my all. I graduated with a First-Class Honours BA in 2004 and totally surprised myself by landing a job as a junior designer in a very successful interior design agency in central London. If I thought university had been terrifying, this was OFF THE SCALE! I was launched into the world of retail design immediately and expected to hit the ground running. I was asked to produce design drawings, concept sketches and to be part of huge project development meetings. I worked in a great team of people but there were some 'characters' and if you didn't come up to scratch, they would certainly let you know. You could say this made me much more resilient but at heart I was fragile, always seeking approval, desperate to convince myself (more than anyone else) that I was worthy of this job.

Now, well into my 20's, I had made it up to the rank of senior designer. I was calmer and more confident, and the mind monkeys had taken a bit of a backseat. However, I was really feeling the pull of motherhood and had wanted a family (probably much more than a career) for as long as I could remember.

Despite a few setbacks my husband and I finally welcomed our first son into the world in 2009. Without any 'proper' discussion about my role going forward I simply made it easy for my employers and left the company. Ultimately, I followed my heart and knew I wanted to be a full-time mum and raise my son without the need of other care. This was wonderful, don't get me wrong, but a big part of me felt that I had let the mind monkeys win. That I had given up my job because of my continued sense of self-doubt assuming motherhood would be an easier option. Yes, I can hear you laughing!

Obviously, motherhood is never the easier option, and I was lucky to have had a partner who gently tried to encourage me back into a career path that could work for our family and restore some of the 'me' that had gone missing. So, in 2010 we set up Laura Porter Interior Design (LPID), deliberating on names and branding we decided, in the end, the company name had to convey its unique selling point – me. I would love to tell you that I spent lots of time researching self-employment, working out 'best practices', getting financial advice and researching competitors. Nope, I did none of that because between dealing with a 1-year-old and renovating our tired and rundown Edwardian home I had zero time to commit.

In the end, the only way to get the business off the ground was to 'Just Do It' I set up a website on a shoestring and managed to get a few friends and contacts to give me a chance to work on their homes for next to nothing. Despite considering myself a very competent interior designer, I had never worked in the residential sector before and in those first few years I really agonised about whether this was the right fit for me. Designing people's homes is so very personal, very different from designing shops, bars, and cafes. But one of the things I know I am good at is being approachable and good at communicating with people. I capitalised on this, I went above and beyond, working far too many hours on certain projects just in

the hope that a good review would lead to more recommendations. Again, I stuck at it… and then my second son was born,
and I had a setback. It didn't seem like a setback at the time as I
was now the proud mum of two beautiful, energetic boys but
the mind monkeys were back: *"Why are you doing this? This is too*
much for you, why don't you just make pretty things, you're much
better at that"

It was true I had begun to try and focus again on my crafty
pursuits and had noticed that suddenly I had people becoming
increasingly interested in my sewing side-line business, maybe I
was better at that? It certainly felt like great work to be doing
around two small boys. I could easily sit on a floor watching
them play while embroidering cushions and no one needed 'site
meetings' to talk about handmade gifts. This business, named
'Laura Lu' absolutely thrived. I was flooded over the next 4
years with requests and made handsewn textile gifts for people
from all over the UK. LPID carried on quietly in the background, but I found myself hiding from the interiors work still
believing that it was too difficult to work around small children.

In 2017 I finally decided that enough was enough, I could no
longer juggle the two businesses and as much as it pained me to
let it go, Laura Lu really had run its course. I had enjoyed those
years of creative fun and it had worked so well alongside my
little boys. But they were growing up, Laura Lu wasn't bringing
in the money we wanted, and I needed to stop making excuses
and go back to the business that I was so scared of.

This decision was probably one of my smartest and bravest
moves. With the children in school everyday I knew I had more
time, I could commit to visiting clients all over Hampshire and
it was time to shine. I threw myself back into LPID, again
working lots of hours, desperate to keep building great recommendations and to broaden my client base to a wider area. I
began to realise that I had to 'invest' in myself and the business.
That I needed to 'walk the walk' to be able to 'talk the talk'. I

smartened myself up, ditched the mum wardrobe, upgraded my design hardware and software. I also started to realise that despite my fierce independence I needed to recognise that I could not do EVERYTHING. I stopped trying to be a graphic designer and brought onboard a brilliant husband and wife team who overhauled my branding and website. I also put myself out there, seeking opportunities to be featured in the press, and do you know what, it worked! Magazines came calling and in 2019 I was featured in three publications.

And while I was doing this the work flowed in. I was receiving weekly enquiries and suddenly my project capacity increased three-fold. Yes, again it was very hard work but when you are giving it your all, there is less time for self-doubt and imposter syndrome. I started mentally 'bottling' the great reviews and lovely feedback, so I had them in the bank for the bad days.

In late 2019 I took on one of the biggest projects I had ever encountered. At first when the enquiry came in I thought "nope, no way, this is too big for me, I will have to politely decline" Luckily for me, I have a very supportive husband who gently asked me to consider it as no different from my more 'standard' projects just with more rooms! So, I said yes, I met them, they were some of the nicest people in the world and we spent the next two years working on their home.

This project was a huge learning curve and I learnt to try not to rush through my projects like I used to at the behest of the mind monkeys *"Quick! Get it done, get paid, before they realise that you are a failure".* I have learnt that in business (and life) building great client relationships takes time but pays massive dividends in the end. By taking on a project that scared me I was able to confront some of my fears about how I operate my business.

The last two years threw my business a huge curveball and

like so many it was fight or flight time. I evolved and have embraced online working despite initially feeling that the business would die if I couldn't 'see' a client in their own home. Instead, video meetings have been fun, engaging and surprisingly easy. I have been able to design from a distance (with a little bit of measuring help from my clients!). In fact this newer way of working has meant that I've been able to offer my design services further afield than I would ever have imagined possible.

My business continues to succeed and now I am in the fortunate position to be booked out months and months in advance. I can't quite believe it when I look back to those early years of frantically feeding babies while searching online for the 'perfect chair' for clients who I thought would hate everything I showed them! I will always progress at a pace I feel comfortable with and stick to my gut instinct which I believe has steered me well this far. If I decide to grow the business further by bringing someone else into the LPID fold I will do it because it feels right and not because the mind monkeys tell me not to!

BIO:

Laura Porter is an experienced interior designer based in Hampshire. After working in the industry for 15 years she offers clients a professional service which is tailored to individual needs. Well-designed and planned interiors enhance the enjoyment we get from our living spaces and Laura takes pride in helping people to reinvigorate and love their homes. *"Every client is unique and designing a space to suit their needs gives me an opportunity to build great working relationships with new people. Seeing a client's reaction to their transformed home is absolutely the most rewarding part of my job."*

www.lauraporter.co.uk

19

DON'T GIVE UP YOUR DAY DREAM

Lisa Gardner

I AM AN ARTIST. Something I say with confidence and passion. But it hasn't always been that way. My relationship with creativity has ebbed and flowed, with self-doubt and self-judgement having their say too. The difference is, now I give myself permission to paint, play and make mistakes with my art.

My story

Today, I have arrived; my sitting bones are connected to the earth; I am waving length along my spine, lifting up through the crown of my head to the sky. Paintbrush in hand, palette teaming with blues, purples, and pinks. This is my time, time for me, time for yoga and time for my creativity. Inhale just, exhale be, inhale just, exhale be … the corners of mouth turn up into a gentle smile, savouring this moment of contentment. A far cry from my thoughts just 7 years earlier…

Back ache, disgruntled, a hot summer's day in 2014 and I am painting Christmas Trees, I am using the 'C' word in summer! A festive palette of red, green, and gold should be joyful. But my reindeers look more like confused cows, and my twinkling lights have lost their twinkle. Hunched over sketch books, inner critic in full flow – 'you will never hit the deadline, Christmas is already ruined' – imposter syndrome wades in to join the thought party – 'they are going to realise you are not a professional artist, they've obviously made a mistake in trusting you'.

I've not taken a break for hours; what is mindfulness? More like a mind full of mess! A half-eaten sandwich cast aside, curling awkwardly like my spine, drying out in the stale air, rough to the touch like the back of my throat. Ending the day tired and uninspired, and already dreading the trip to the studio the next day. I've worked so hard for my dream job, but today it doesn't feel so dreamy.

I'd been practising yoga for a while, but it was something that stayed on my mat. That sacred me time, reserved for that space. Yoga was a reset button, and I hadn't started to translate its teachings into my daily life. One blustery, English summer's evening I'd made it to class in the rain (an achievement in itself; the temptation to stay home had been strong!), sat on my mat, and it occurred to me, while here I was happy. It didn't matter what else was going on; I wanted to bottle this feeling up and let it spill out into the other areas of my life, in particular my art studio.

The experiment began and, very importantly, I invited play into my work. I had a sudden curiosity to colour outside the lines! Paint bigger, bolder, and not worry about perfect pictures. Just as I had stopped striving for perfect postures on the mat, my art was now taking on a new shape. I still had my deadlines but taking mindful breaks during the day to stretch and to notice my breath had a huge impact on my wellbeing and, therefore, on my work. The more I practised my Pranayama (breath meditations), the more accepting I was of making mistakes. Mistakes lead to those 'beautiful oops' moments that can only be found when things don't go to plan.

My concept for Watercolour Wellbeing was emerging: a workshop that draws on the teachings of my art and yoga. As my own authentic practice was evolving, I was driven to share this creative union. Warming up my mind and my body was helping me access my creativity in a new way. It wasn't another thing to add to my 'to do' list; it was a natural evolution of me as an artist. I felt strong; I was compelled to trust my gut and listen to my heart. 7 years on I start each artwork with a movement meditation to warm up my body, flowing arms and wrists mean flowing brushstrokes. A breath meditation follows to calm my mind and centre myself, and to tap into my creative intuition. I allow myself to explore, and I create the time for fun in my work. It's easy to get caught up in the glorification of busy, but taking short mindful breaks and giving myself permission to go off on an artistic tangent has accelerated my art and my wellbeing. My art and yoga practice run parallel to each other; taking the decision to train to be a Yoga teacher in 2018 was the confidence tipping point that unified my profession. There is a beautiful Sanskrit word – Lila (pronounced Lee-la) – which translates as divine play, and this word is never far from my mind. We can all benefit from more playtime. By adopting this mindset with our work we remove our self-imposed barriers.

So please, don't give up on your day dream – my day dream led me to Watercolour Wellbeing, and here I am getting ready to celebrate my third year, working with nature conservation charities, private clients and launching a body of art work that I am beyond proud of.

Breathe with your paint brush

To help you invite play into your life and to encourage a balanced mind in your business, I have included this watercolour experiment for you to add to your own wellbeing tool kit.

You will need:

- A4 paper (preferably cartridge or watercolour)
- Watercolour paint (pencils can be used as a replacement)
- Paintbrush
- Water Jar

Ocean Breath

When the Ocean is restless it can be hard to see the horizon. When the waves are calm all becomes clear. This is the same with our minds. Pranayama (prah-nah-yah-mah) in yoga means breathing meditation. Let's practice this Pranayama together:

- Sit or stand with ease.
- Wave length up your spine, all the way through to the crown of your head.
- Observe the natural, rhythmic flow of your breath.
- Invite softness into your jaw.
- Inhale and exhale through your nose.
- With your thoughts inspired by the ocean, paint the bottom two-thirds of the page with water.
- Inhale and bathe your brush with colour, have a palette of colours to hand.
- Exhale long sweeping brush strokes horizontally across the full length of the page, perhaps adding a wave like motion (paper can be portrait or landscape).
- Continue for cycles of up to nine breaths at a time.
- Allow space between each brushstroke, invite the page to breathe with you.

• Pause and watch the paint saturate your canvas. While the paint is flowing, become immersed in your art.

• Notice how you feel.

When we mindfully observe our inhale, and our exhale, it becomes a meditation. Meditation brings your awareness to one thing. It's a simple concept, but just because it's simple doesn't mean it's easy. Painting is a tool we can employ to connect us to this present moment, helping us quieten the background hum of busy thoughts. By inviting our canvas to breathe with us, we can pause, enjoy watching the paint dance, and become joyfully immersed in the process. Many embrace the benefits of meditation – you too can enjoy an increase in your attention span, a feeling of connection, a reduction in your stress levels and a boost to your immune system. The word inspiration literally translates as breathing in, so let us breathe in, be inspired and let our passions lead the way to a joyous life.

My hope for you

Life and art have been easier and more enjoyable since I've allowed myself to be guided by my own instinctive rhythm. I'm often asked what first planted the seeds of my art. My answer is simple: it has always been a part of who I am. Art is my therapy, and it is this deeply intuitive, sensitive, and healing energy that I strive to embed into every single piece I create. Whether I'm telling the story behind the language of flowers, capturing emotions through the dance of a paintbrush, or breathing life into an environment that needs to be cherished, my pieces balance beauty and meaning, presence and reflection. But it is the creative process that really sets my work free. It is the intricate culmination of breath, meditation, and movement ... a pyramid of inner indulgence that opens the doors to my soul sanctuary. To me, this offers the portal to a truly joyful and liberated journey.

My hope for you is that you, too, find your inner rhythm so you can live and work in flow with it. Fighting against it to fit an external ideal is exhausting, but beautiful things happen when we really connect with and nurture our innate healing energies.

BIO:

Lisa Gardner delivers regular Watercolour Wellbeing classes online and in-person across Hampshire – Watercolour Wellbeing classes explore free flowing painting techniques & breathing meditations to nurture your creativity and inspire calm. She is a watercolour artist inspired by the natural world, the connection between breath and brushwork and the utter joy that can be found when paint meets the canvas. From her studio on the south coast of England, Lisa crafts whimsical artwork under the name Iris Hill – an homage to her Nan, the woman who lit Lisa's creative flame and helped it burn bright. She has collaborated with organisations from around the world – including Arts Council England, Hampshire Cultural Trust, Plantlife and Child and Adolescent Mental Health Services and has had her work sold as limited editions in Belle Art Gallery – Bondi, Australia. Her free flowing paintings have also adorned yoga studios, family therapy rooms and been featured on Carte Blanche and Gemma International greeting cards. But her greatest achievement? Doing what she loves on a daily basis and sharing that love with other people. In her own words, "I believe passionately that I deserve the right to live a creative life that feels extraordinary. I want to share that gift with as many people for as long as possible."

www.irishill.co.uk

20

THE ADVENTURES OF GOING WITH
THE FLOW

Lynda Fussell

L ife is full of ups and downs and the magic comes from riding with the waves and not resisting. Going with the flow.

I used to think that my CV was like a checkerboard and that it was a bad thing. Years later, I realise that the experiences have all added to 'me', the person who lives my life.

Over the years I have done many things, had many opportunities and plenty of adventures as I followed husbands around the world. Yeah, plural husbands, but that is another story!

The continual movement into new and exciting places meant that my career path was adaptive and evolving. When living remotely on an air force base near the Kruger Park, in South Africa, I had the joy of setting up my first horse riding school, teaching local families about the joy and confidence of being with horses. This business followed me in various guises for many years until I left Africa.

Why did I teach horse riding? I was an experienced rider, trained instructor, had my own horses, rescued more horses, and had a willing captive market who wanted to ride and learn. Perfect!

Every business since then has been the result of being open to what is naturally around me and is inspiring. Something that fuels my curiosity and that I am willing to explore. Not everything works out as expected but everything surely evolves so long as I go with the flow and keep curious enough to explore potential ideas.

Corporate life at the turn of the century

Years later, when living back in Johannesburg after many adventures in Africa and Europe, I was deep into corporate life, wearing suits, working hard, and playing harder. 2000 was a huge event for those of us involved in anything that depended on technology coping with the turn of the century. What a time that was …

We sailed into the twenty-first century and breathed a sigh of relief. I had my own office, a secretary who looked after me and my diary, and a boss, who had a boss, etc. Pay was good. Stress, attitudes, and behaviours were poor! Sexism, elitism, and the like.

I took the standard three-week holiday abroad, enjoying sun and fun in Tenerife and Spain with my girls and my best friend from school. On that holiday, I woke up. I realised that this was life. I had been existing, not living, and I wasn't willing to continue like that. I returned and resigned – boom!

Working on my terms

I sat quietly for six weeks ignoring all the calls from those who thought I had completely 'lost it'. I looked at what made me happy. What I liked doing. Who I liked spending time with. Who I respected in the work environment. And I started talking to people who wanted my advice, my insights, my expertise and who valued me. I needed to set up a business, and quickly, as I had work that was on my terms.

I felt so lucky and was so grateful for the life that I was now *living*. I was able to dictate what assignments I chose to accept, and developed various specialist programmes and offers I could leverage. Each conversation opened up other opportunities. I was always open to exploring but conscious of what I valued – mostly the people and reason behind the work.

Things evolved into a partnership with three other people and suddenly I was in a much bigger business. We got involved in mergers and became real players in the industry.

And then, once again, I looked at what was really important to me. My family. As a single mum I knew I wanted to return to the United Kingdom so that my girls could have the opportunities and support of the English schooling system.

Doing what's best for my girls

So I made plans to leave my businesses, friends, and associates and return to England with no real plan but the confidence that anything was possible. I knew that with faith, curiosity and focus I could start again. So we packed up and moved – single mum and two young girls, no job, no fixed destination, no real plan, just amazing friends who provided space for me to once again explore, think, talk to people, reconnect with previous colleagues and work out what next.

I must be the luckiest person in the world. A friend from my former corporate work life in Surrey connected me with my next boss. I landed a fabulous job with a consultancy company and spent longer there than in any job to date. Seven and half years later, in the aftermath of the 2008 banking crisis, assignments in Yorkshire were pretty thin and I was asked to work in Southampton for 12 months.

I chose to decline as I couldn't see how I could work away from my youngest daughter doing her A-levels and be even further from my other daughter who was in her first year at university in Aberystwyth. My role as a mother was to support my girls and this assignment didn't fit.

Once again, I was looking for opportunities, exploring options, talking to people I knew, liked, and trusted. I got the opportunity to do a short piece of consulting work in Bradford, which was pretty local, and just the kind of work I liked. I needed to set up a business to invoice for this work and suddenly I was a business owner once again. This work developed into four years of magic. Great people, culture, and projects.

Eleven years on and I am still evolving and exploring and loving life with this same business. I have been lucky to secure amazing contracts all over the world. I've had fun. I've developed and gained confidence. I've worked bloomin' hard and I've been reminded about life when you don't follow your truth.

Context

The details I've not expounded but which provide some context, include working in health insurance as a broker, adviser, and administrator. Running the marketing department in a sizeable business. Project and programme management for technology and business change projects in financial services, utilities, retail, and public service. My life and career has been varied, hence my checkerboard reference at the beginning... I have seen things, experienced situations, people, leaders, life events both amazing and pretty grim. They have all shaped my world and perspectives, and for that I am very grateful. Throughout my journey I have continued to study, seek more, understand how and why – mostly in the way we operate as people. What is now called personal development was just a mashup of books, stories, courses, and discussions for many years. I listened to the elders. I learnt from trailblazers. I was inherently curious about life, and the human mind, emotions, and relationships.

Unexpected changes

I did one challenging assignment that really shook my world and caused me to pause again. I sought refuge for a week in a lovely retreat venue that I had located a few months earlier. They were running a coach training course. Blah blah, what is all that about? I had many friends who were coaches, but I wasn't really sure what they did. I had a hectic, busy, high-powered 'real' job after all, didn't I? The venue lured me. The timing was perfect being a week after finishing that grim assignment. A week in the most amazing place and a certification thrown in too, who wouldn't? I signed up and my life changed once more, completely unexpectedly. In the first hour on the first day, I was perplexed. Is this what coaches do? But I've been doing this for years. 'People' is my game. Every successful business, every project, every encounter, involves motivating people through creating trust and the environment for them to thrive. This was what I had learnt many years back and had employed in my world from right back to my school days through every role and encounter since.

I loved the course. We worked so hard and were busy from 7am to 11pm. We studied, discussed, did role plays (which I hate) and yet I thrived. I was inspired. I was energised. I was rejuvenated and ready to go out there once more and do something else...

After finally qualifying and doing the assessment hours and thesis, I tentatively reached out, and people came. I had something new. For the next few years I continued to consult and do private coaching part time. It felt like the perfect balance. As things got busier on both aspects, I had to make a decision and looked to expand the business with associates and different models. Suddenly I was in a whole different ball game and exploring once again.

My girls were both married and settled in their lives, so I had space to try new things and have some fun. I started running retreats, I loved going on them so why not create them? Things can change in an instant, sometimes as a result of your actions and sometimes due to external factors. The Covid-19 pandemic arrived, and everything changed. I withdrew my January and February 2020 retreats while we waited to see what was really happening. What a fabulous opportunity to step back and reflect, once again, on what matters most, what makes you happy and what others might value from you. With a now extensive toolkit, there were so many options and opportunities.

What I've learnt

These days I enjoy the balance of consulting, working with my local NHS Trust, running training courses and coaching. It has been a journey to this point, and it certainly isn't over yet. What life has shown me is the incredible ability we all have to survive and thrive. We adapt. We grow. We evolve. With a curious mindset and good people to hold space for us to explore we are amazing. I know I need to have fun and to have time to do the simple things – my daily yoga, long walks, time with friends, and especially time with my family. My family has always been my main 'why' and nothing has changed. My girls have their own families, and I am honoured to be able to share their journeys with them. My parents are getting older, and we find new things to do together.

Having the choice of the work I do, the way I do it and keeping my values at the forefront allows my life to ebb and flow through the changes. I desire unlimited energy and excitement for life, my family and all the children. I focus on bringing clarity, confidence, and joy to the people I encounter throughout each and every day. I choose to be happy and continue having adventures.

BIO:

Lynda Fussell is a coach and healer who works with clients all over the world. Individuals, small business owners and corporate teams all benefit from Lynda's support and guidance which is backed by years of coaching and mentoring. Her range of experience across industries, businesses and countries positions Lynda with a unique ability and insight to support leaders as they grow and develop in their roles, while navigating the complexities of home life and personal satisfaction.

Interspersed with the coaching activities Lynda has continued to spend time doing corporate consultancy in the fields of change management, innovation, and communications. Listening is one of her chief skills. Talking is her natural instinct. Writing is a passion and a way to share stories for more people to access.

Lynda lives in the spa town of Harrogate, in North Yorkshire, England, which provides the perfect backdrop for her adventures, retreats, walking and yoga getaways, plus the global coaching and consulting assignments.

Life is filled with the magic of nature and happy people.

All our experiences shape our adventures and experiences.

www.lyndafussell.com

21

DO WHAT YOU LOVE AND DO LOTS OF IT

Jennifer Jones

Everyone is different, and that's what makes us great. The same goes for the word 'success'. It means different things to each of us, which makes it exciting. Wouldn't it be boring if everyone was identical, and everyone strived for the same thing?

When I was growing up, I was always encouraged to be successful and the older I got, the more I realised that my version of success differed wildly from those around me. I was urged to earn as much money as possible and have a career in a widely recognised profession like law or accountancy. The focus was always on money, money, money, and I think that was because having lots of money, no matter what you were doing, was considered successful. I didn't know why that never sat well with me. When I started to climb the corporate ladder and earn more money, I realised what the problem was.

The lightbulb moment

I hit a wall in my corporate career and hired a life coach (best thing I ever did!) to figure out why I wasn't happy although I was earning great money and had a well-respected career. That's when the lightbulb moment happened … I didn't love my job. I didn't feel successful because I wasn't fulfilled. I wasn't excited by what I was doing, which was holding me back.

That was the turning point – the moment I said enough is enough. I needed to decide what success meant to me. After digging deep to really understand what made me tick, what put a smile on my face, and what I wanted to achieve in life, I discovered it: personal styling!

I LOVE fashion, shopping, and helping others feel good. I put all these things together and ta-da! That's how I found my new career. That's how I discovered what my niche was and what I was meant to do. I know that sounds cheesy, and if I had read that ten years ago, I'd have thought the same; but now I believe there's something we're all meant to do, we just some-times need help finding out what it is. Sometimes people go through life not ever finding it (sounds like I'm writing a romance novel here) and that's okay for some. But it wasn't for me. I don't think I would've ever been content if I didn't discover my real passion.

And now, five years later, I have no regrets.

So what do I do? In short, it's personal styling, but there's so much more to it. I help mums (and I'll come on to why I specialise in helping mums soon) go from self-conscious to style confident.

When you become a mum, your relationship with fashion and clothes can change. With little time to focus on yourself and the ever-changing needs children have as they grow and develop, our wardrobes are no longer our priority. But like they say – happy mum, happy baby/children – so making time for yourself and feeling good in what you wear is important.

In my job, I get to see mums go from feeling fed up with what they see in the mirror, to having the biggest smile on their face because they've fallen back in love with themselves. That's what brings me the most joy. And that's not all, I also help other women, like myself, follow their dreams. I provide in-depth personal styling training courses that enable others to pursue a rewarding and flexible career.

Listen to your little voice

We all have that little voice inside our heads, so if yours is urging you to find your success, like mine did, please listen to it. Don't ignore it or put it to one side to come back to later. Explore it and see where it takes you. You never know what could happen, what adventure it could take you on.

I know that running a business isn't for everyone. It takes hard work, dedication, and belief in yourself. It also requires constant learning and self-development. Does that put you off? If it doesn't and those things sound like you, then you're perfect for the job.

There are parts of running a business that you might not enjoy (you can't get away from that), but if it's a business that you're passionate about and you love what you do, you'll want to do lots of it. Half the time you can't drag yourself away from it. It's your baby; you've built it from the ground up. That's what drives you and what makes those little bits you don't like to do, worth doing.

Be prepared to put in the hours

I might have made going from working in a corporate world to having your own successful business sound easy. And while it hasn't felt particularly difficult, it's taken a lot of hard work. It didn't happen overnight.

When I found my niche, I took time to explore working with personal styling clients and gaining as much experience as possible, building up my reputation and putting things in place to help my clients find me, such as my website and social media, all alongside keeping the security of my day job. And this meant working long hours – sometimes all week, most evenings, and weekends. There was a period when I worked my 9–5 all week and then worked in John Lewis' personal styling department on the weekends. This was all in aid of building up my confidence and figuring out what kind of stylist I wanted to be.

I wish I'd written down the hours I spent working on my business to get everything ready for launch because I think it would be a shocking statistic. But the funny thing is, when I look back on that time, it was tiring but I also loved every minute of it.

I can have it all

When I discovered personal styling, it was so obviously right for me, but I was nervous. I didn't think a career in fashion was accessible to me, especially after being in a corporate environment for so long. It never occurred to me that I could start again and learn a new skill, but I did. It's never too late.

Although starting my business was exciting and I wanted to share it with the world, others were sceptical: "Is that a proper job? How can you earn what you earn now shopping for people? Surely you can't get paid to dress people?" And I still hear that now. But that's other people's ideas of success, not mine. For me success was building a career doing something I loved and making a huge difference to other people's lives. And now I am doing just that!

I'm being paid to dress people and shop for a living. I'm doing a job I love, helping mums rediscover their confidence while juggling my own mum-life.

I think a lot of women worry about whether they can have it all – can you run a successful business, have a family, and still have a social life? Before I had my son, Jacob, I was of the view of "how hard can it be?", which is when I started my business. Then, when I fell pregnant, I panicked – how am I going to have maternity leave and not lose all the progress I'd made in building my business? Then when I had Jacob ... mind blown! I had to adapt, and I hired a stylist to look after my clients during this period.

On reflection, I realised taking a step back actually helped me move forwards. During my maternity leave, I was able to think even more about what I loved doing in my business and who I loved working with, while simultaneously experiencing the same challenges my clients have with their wardrobes when they have a family. My relationship with fashion changed. My body shape changed, there were certain things I didn't want to wear anymore, and I needed to be more conscious of having practical clothing. I used my skills as a stylist to get back on track with my style, potentially quicker than others might do, which motivated me more to help other mums get back to feeling like them again.

That's when I realised how my business can really help mums, even more than I'd thought previously. When Jacob was just six months old, I eased into styling again, and Covid-19 hit – the timing of it all! But like many other women entrepreneurs, I adapted once again. I took everything online to keep the business going and continued to help mums virtually, until things began to get back to normal.

To recap, I asked the question of can you have it all? After becoming a mum, I had some serious doubts. I struggled to see how I was going to juggle everything, but that's when I really saw the flexibility that having a business can bring. You do work lots of hours, but you can choose your hours. If I want to spend an afternoon with my family rather than work,

I can. So, my answer: yes – without a doubt you can have it all.

I'm so proud to be where I am now – I get to style amazing women every day and give them the confidence to wear what they love, and love what they see in the mirror. I went from having no experience in the fashion industry, to running my own personal styling company, working one-on-one with clients, training other stylists, and expanding my company. Yes, it was scary, but I don't regret a thing: I love what I do, and I do lots of it!

I know many women feel stuck in a career rut, just how my clients feel about their wardrobes, but haven't yet found the courage to take that leap of faith and start afresh. If that sounds like you, follow my example: it's possible! You can follow your dreams and be successful. And if you think personal styling could also be the right career for you, then feel free to give me a shout – I'd love to have a chat about it.

On to the next styling chapter

Okay, so I've told you a lot about me; I've told you how far I've come – from a cog in the corporate machine, to a blossoming entrepreneur. But what's next for Jennifer Jones Styling? I sometimes have so many ideas, it's hard to know which path to follow, and I guess that's what comes with being successful in business – you can't wait to start the next venture. We do have to reign that in sometimes though and make sure we're making the best choices.

I definitely see growth in my future. I see more stylists working with me and my team to spread the love of rebuilding your confidence through what you wear. I will do what I love for as long as I can. I want to continue empowering mums with the skills and knowledge to shop with confidence and dress with style.

. . .

BIO:

Jennifer truly believes that every mum deserves to feel confident, powerful, and beautiful. She will help you find a style you love, that's perfectly suited to you and will not only make you look amazing, it will make you feel like you can take on the world.

Jennifer helps you find the right clothing to do just that, no matter what you're juggling in your daily life. Her team of friendly stylists take you from self-conscious to style confident and help you fall in love with your wardrobe again. Using her knowledge of designers, shops, boutiques, colours, and silhouettes, we help you find a comfortable, effortlessly chic style that perfectly fits your personality and lifestyle. She also provides personal styling training courses that are ideal for those interested in starting their career in personal styling.

www.jenniferjonestyling.com

22

MANIFESTING MY DREAM

Maddy Alexander-Grout

When I moved back to Southampton 12 years ago, I was 40k in debt from uni – I'd got myself into a bit of a mess with credit cards, overdrafts and loans. I didn't understand money at 18, and when I was given some freedom, I went a bit nuts, so to speak.

At freshers' fair I was like a kid in a sweet shop! FREE money! whoop! or so I thought, I signed up for every credit card, bank account and loan going.

Pubs and nights out every night; I bought ALL of the clothes Leicester had to offer. Within about 4 months of starting my first year I was skint.

I got a job and had to work all the hours under the sun. I neglected my course and felt depressed all the time. I went to the university hardship fund and got a grant: I blew that.

I got another loan, and I was spiralling.

In 2004 I left university, penniless without a degree and in a whole load of trouble with the debts I'd racked up. I tried to run from them and buried my head in the sand. They'd never find me in a new city!

WRONG! The letters started to come. Threats from bailiffs – some even came to my house and took my things.

I got a job and started to earn some decent money. I got a debit card specifically for people with bad credit: I couldn't even pay in shops with it. All I could do was get out cash, a certain amount each week.

I was forced to learn how to budget by this card scheme I was on, but I didn't learn. Instead, I started to use sites like Wonga to get money fast. My debt spiral was insane, and in 2008 I had to turn to family for support. My mum helped me to write a budget plan.

In 2011 I was at my lowest. I lost all my possessions in a house fire. I lost my job. My friends started to call me "jobless mc homeless" (in a jokey way but it still hurt).

Things had to change

I worked hard and started to pay off my debts, this time vowing to myself I would never get myself in trouble again and that I would live within my means.

In 2012 I started my own business, a recruitment agency in Southampton. It flopped because I still hadn't got to grips with my spending, and I couldn't get to grips with how to get my business visible (that is another story).

I had to go back to the world of work, but that was ok. I worked my way up in the HR world, and the more I earned the more I paid off. But I was always so resentful of friends who had money. Working in HR, I learnt about employee benefits, and by 2014 I was debt free finally!

In December 2014 I had repaired my credit rating enough to buy a house! Eek! I bought a shared ownership two-bed house. I was really excited about having friends to stay and it being a nice summer garden party type house.

A shock to the system

In January 2015 I found out I was pregnant, which was a huge shock as I had previously been told I wouldn't be able to have children. Overwhelmed, my first thought was holy crap! How am I going to afford a baby? What if I get into debt again?

Eight months of ailments followed: gestational diabetes, cholestasis, rib flare, dagger crotch (dont ask!). And then a scary labour, a week in hospital due to low blood sugar and jaundice. I was already a mess when I took my newborn home.

I am the sort of mum who lives for sleep. I love an afternoon nap for no reason. I love lie ins. I also like drinking and socialising and having a newborn came as a shock, as it does to most people, but my baby cried ALL THE TIME.

Finding support

I didn't know what to do; he was just so cross. I started a parenting forum because I felt alone. I didn't have anyone to talk to and I didn't know where to turn. I began to get sick; I would have visions of throwing my newborn baby down the stairs or us getting hit by a car.

I didn't know what was real, and I genuinely felt like I was living in a parallel universe. My mum noticed I wasn't myself and suggested I go to the doctors. My doctor said I had post-natal depression and tried to prescribe me tablets. I wasn't interested; I started to be fearful of leaving the house. I felt like I was being judged by other parents. I thought they knew what I was thinking and knew I had visions of killing my child.

I knew I was losing it. I went to see a therapist who diagnosed me with a condition called postpartum psychosis. I got some help, luckily before it was too late, and I did something stupid.

I also found out why Ben cried so much: he had a compressed neck muscle and was in a lot of pain. This was easily sorted by the lovely Alex Lys, a local cranial osteopath (and now partner offering discounts).

The parents I met through the parenting forum I'd set up were amazing and actually the least judgemental people, but I knew I still wanted to help more parents, so I kept the forum running. Local businesses started to contact me about advertising; I wanted to help them too, but I didn't know how.

A VIP birth

Ben never really slept properly and one sleepless night in July 2017 I had an idea which would change my life. What if I could have a discount card that supported local businesses and helped parents to save money?

I'd kept on top of my debts but eating so much coffee and cake with my mummy friends was starting to take its toll on my maternity leave salary.

I started to contact local businesses offering them free advertising in exchange for a discount. Everyone I spoke to thought it was a fab idea, and after four months of plugging away in my spare time, I had 80 parent-related discounts to start off my card! I wanted to call it My VIP Card – the VIP originally stood for "Very Important Parent".

We launched on 30 November 2017 with just a Facebook page. By February I'd sold 200 subscriptions and we were growing the offers daily. I decided it was time for a website! So I reinvested the money I'd made to get a website. People loved it but wanted more, and it was so hard to do everything on my own, so I took on a virtual assistant. Katie was the best thing to happen to my business, she was honestly the glue that kept me together.

I started to network in my spare time, and on learning I'd be made redundant in April 2018, I decided this was worth fighting for. I didn't look for another job, I did a temp job for a bit but then found out I was pregnant again.

Growth

This time it was sort of planned. I wanted another one, but I was really scared about how it would affect the business which was just starting to build momentum! Also, I'd just agreed a partnership to offer national offers alongside my local Hampshire offers.

In November 2018 I won the Hampshire Women's Business of the Year award! This really pushed me forward with articles in local and national press and an interview with BBC Radio Solent.

I had a huge blip in my mental health after that. I suffered with imposter syndrome and felt I didn't deserve to be successful.

My world changed at a networking event when I saw a wonderful inspiring lady give a talk about manifesting. She gave me a small cube of rose quartz which I've kept in my bra ever since. My imposter syndrome went away, and I started to manifest what I wanted for the business.

In February 2019 I gave birth to my beautiful daughter Harriet. The pregnancy had its fair share of complications, but I decided to plough on without maternity leave. Instead, Harriet came with me to corporate meetings, networking, and awards ceremonies. She was the best networked baby in Hampshire and helped to get me noticed.

I continued to grow the business and decided to franchise and go nationwide with our offers. We signed up over 2300 businesses across the UK and made it so that My VIP Card helped you to shop local wherever you go, helping hospitality, leisure and small businesses nationwide.

Covid and crowdfunding

Covid hit us hard. We instantly lost all our sales. No one could use our discounts, so we ploughed our energy into helping businesses to stay visible. I manifested daily; we crowd-funded to support our suppliers and make sure they got paid and supported others. We then did an equity crowdfunding campaign and raised 84k and got another 150k worth of investment from angel investors.

Crowdfunding is the hardest thing I have ever done to date. I couldn't have done it without my operations manager Nicola Toner. Also manifesting! It sounds crazy but it works! I opened myself up to the universe and it gave me what I wanted.

We now have 246 shareholders, which is amazing! I knew I had to use the money to make our product strong to go into a new (hopefully Covid-free) world!

We hadn't been just a card for quite some time, so we decided to change our name and rebrand the whole business over the last six months. It's been really tough but I haven't lost sight of our end goal.

We've just relaunched as My VIP Rewards, the money saving app that helps to reward people and community with a different business model to the franchise.

We now have over 5000 offers on our new app, so people can save money on anything and everything, from supermarket shopping to days out, and most importantly, it continues my mission to support small independent businesses across the UK.

New directions

The Southampton parenting forum has grown to a huge 7.9k members and I had the idea to help even more parents – crazy I know, but that gave me the idea for business number two!

I'm creating an app very similar to Facebook to support parents from when they're trying to conceive through to kids flying the nest! It's called Parenthood App, and by the time you read this it should be live! Eek!

My journey from being penniless and homeless to debt free and running a business valued at £1.8 million has been such a learning curve. But I want to inspire people. I didn't come from a business background, and I've learnt everything I know from networking and connecting with others, believing in myself and being resilient as hell.

No parent is perfect, especially not me, but working mums totally rock. We aren't given enough credit. So if you're reading this and thinking about starting a business... just do it and manifest the sh*t out of it, work hard and don't give up!

BIO:

Maddy Alexander-Grout is a mum of two Ben (6) and Harriet (2). She and her children live with her husband James and dog Dexter in Shirley, Southampton. When she's not working, she loves reading crime dramas, crafting, and going to festivals. She's also a bit of a gin fanatic. She runs two businesses: My VIP Rewards and Parenthood App. Maddy's been a radio presenter most of her life, and she hosts a podcast called the VIP Cast. She loves networking and can often be found running rooms on Clubhouse.

www.myviprewards.co.uk

23

REMEMBER TO LOOK UP

Nicola Webster

I never thought I'd be a person who'd reply to the question 'who do you work for?' with 'I work for myself. I run my own business'.

I'd always been happy being an employee. I enjoyed being part of a team, having people to share the highs (and lows) with, and the social life that came with it too. I'd spent time working in brand licensing at large and medium sized companies, and I'd relished the buzz and excitement that came with working in central London. I worked predominantly on character and entertainment brands, helping to grow and building them through licensing. It involved working closely with companies across different sectors, especially toys, publishing, and apparel. No two days were the same, and licensing is an industry many people are unaware of, though it touches many aspects of our everyday lives.

Big changes

Life didn't stand still, and after moving back to Hampshire (where I grew up), the next change happened when I went on maternity leave in 2015. It was planned that I'd return to work a year later, most likely with a reduction in hours. But just before that time was up, I had a call. Things were changing, my team was being restructured, and I was offered redundancy. I was really torn. It was a job I enjoyed but many of the core team I worked with were leaving and so after a lot of deliberation, I decided to leave.

I took a job with another company. While I enjoyed many aspects of it, it wasn't working for me, and I was left wondering if I'd made the right decision. It was hard to tell whether it was the role that was wrong, or whether my own outlook and ambition had changed since becoming a parent. I carried on for a while and then went on maternity leave for the second time. As that maternity leave drew to an end, I was listening to a podcast about the late Stephen Hawking. It concluded with a quotation from him about remembering to look up at the stars and not down at your feet and this really resonated with me.

*"Remember to look up at the stars and not down at your feet ...
However difficult life may seem, there is always something you can do
and succeed at. It matters that you don't just give up"*
Stephen Hawking

It's an oft told tale, but the juggle of a working mum and the guilt that comes with it, is a challenge. I love being with my children, but I also hadn't worked hard for several years to just throw that career away. People kept telling me that the children would only be young once and that I wouldn't get the time back, but I also knew there were only so many toddler groups and coffee mornings I wanted to go to each week. It's a strange thing losing your identity, you become known as so-and-so's mum rather than you, identified by your child rather than what you do.

I kept coming back to the quotation, and realised I needed to change something. I couldn't carry on plodding along and looking at my feet. It was time to move on, to look up at the stars and dream big.

I needed something different

I was torn. I didn't want to spend a lot of time commuting and miss out on being with my children. I didn't want to be the mum who was never at the school gates. International travel was great, but with kids it became a logistical challenge, and I found myself wanting a different sort of working routine.

I signed up for a course with Digital Mums. My licensing background meant I'd worked closely with marketing and social media teams, and the latter was a growing area I was keen to learn more about. The Digital Mums mission is to help women find work that works for them and their families. This really appealed to me – I truly believed there had to be a way to make a career and parenthood fit together.

Studying again was a shock. I'd taken a few non-assessed evening courses and some professional qualifications since finishing university, but nothing particularly full on. Going back to being a student was another level – I suddenly doubted myself as it was all so different with lots of new platforms, software, and teaching methods.

But once I settled in, I loved it. I had a brilliant peer group; we all spoke daily and have become friends, despite the physical distance between us all. I really enjoyed getting back into learning and found my creativity and enthusiasm again. I was inspired and reminded of the me that wasn't "just" a mum.

The big question remained though, and that was what would

come next. I finally decided to take the risk, wrote my resignation letter, and went freelance.

Learning curves

While the actual work is important, the biggest learning curve about setting up your own business is that you are on your own! There is no IT helpdesk. No finance team. No legal team. No team assistant. It's just you.

I'd been involved in loads of projects that had started with a drawing board (quite literally in many cases), but there'd always been a team to make the decisions. This was the first time I'd had to decide every single thing and not just on client work, but on the business itself. While that was daunting, it was, and still is, tremendously exciting. There are no rights holders or stakeholders to present to; I can make all decisions myself and take risks if I want to.

I listened to other freelancers and took things slowly. The WHY for starting my business is my family. I wanted to spend time with my children and look back with no regrets. I didn't want to miss out on big moments by being stuck on a plane or in a conference centre somewhere.

I went freelance in the summer of 2019, and carefully planned the first six months to give myself a bit of a break, to settle my eldest into Year R (primary school) and deliver the first project I'd taken on.

Everything ground to a halt

All was going well; I built my website, created my brand, joined local and industry networking groups and began building my business. And then exactly six months after I started, the UK went into lockdown in March 2020, and everything ground to a halt.

Like so many other small business owners and freelancers, I panicked. I had never expected to earn in my first few months and had planned for this. But what I hadn't expected was that just as I was reaching the point of taking on new clients, that the world would turn upside down. There was no childcare. No school. No networking opportunities.

With the benefit of hindsight, the timing of the pandemic has been a benefit. Once the initial shock passed, it allowed me to step back and work out what direction to take my business. On a personal level, it meant I was able to be with my children. We learnt how to homeschool. We played, walked, baked, laughed, and sometimes cried. I remembered my why, that I wanted more family time, and I took comfort that I was able to be with my family and we all stayed safe and well.

Taking stock and making plans

The enforced stop period in 2020 allowed me to really work out the direction I wanted to go in. And it's exciting. I now know who my ideal client is, and I've spent a lot of time working on my business. I've invested in more training and built relationships with a network of other freelancers, giving me the support network of a team that I so enjoyed when I was employed.

My business is still small and still very new. Although it's two years since I officially started it, that includes three national lockdowns, with long periods of home schooling and no child-care. In many ways it's still the first year and just the beginning! I have plans to grow the business, some of these will be possible when my youngest starts school and others are more ambitious long-term plans. At the time of writing, it is summer 2021 and it feels like I am starting to achieve the balance of work with having a young family, and I am optimistic that I have found "work that works".

I'm really excited to see what the next phase of my journey as a freelancer will be. I intend to keep looking up to the stars and moving forward, and I hope that my story inspires you to do the same.

BIO:

Nicola Webster has two young daughters and lives in Winchester, Hampshire. She has worked for more than 13 years in brand licensing, on brands within the toy, publishing, media, and technology industries, working both in house and as an agent. She's created successful commercial product ranges and worked on diverse projects in the UK and internationally and has been part of award-winning teams and worked with many well-known brands, personalities and retailers.

In her business, she combines her background and expertise in licensing and branding with continued training in social media to work with businesses and brands to help them tell their story. This ranges from small, local businesses who need help creating and implementing a marketing strategy, to training teams at larger organisations on fitting social media into their wider marketing plans.

She's part of the Social Mums team and runs regular social media workshops – online and in-person (in Hampshire). Nicola is also proud to be a member of groups supporting business owners both locally and nationally, including Hampshire Women's Business Group and Digital Women. She continues to learn and update her skills and is a Facebook Blueprint badge holder.

www.njwebster.com

24

HOW I REALISED MY DREAM IN A PANDEMIC!

Ros Thompson

There are few people who can truly thank Covid-19 for anything; thankfully I am one of the lucky ones and I can say thank you. This is a brief glimpse of how I went from the corporate world to being a full-time Holistic Therapist and living my dream.

At the beginning of 2020, my life was comparatively normal – there were vague words on the news about the unknown word "Coronavirus", but just vague murmurings. I was working full time for an office services provider in Croydon, was travelling circa 2500 miles per month, suited and booted and working in a busy corporate world.

During January 2020 the need to travel to London and to other offices was gradually diminishing, and with the talk of the virus, people weren't welcoming visitors and the word "Zoom" entered my life – I had a large client base of companies working within the care industry and became very involved in the provision of PPE. It was tough and incredibly busy. I spent time talking to nursing and care homes who had lost residents and staff to this new virus; their main aim was to find PPE and my task was to get it for them. Right to the end of March 2020 I was up to my neck in the chaos, the trauma and terror of this near unknown virus, little did I know that furlough was about to evolve and my holistic dream about to come to life.

I had started my holistic journey in 1998, when I was introduced to the wonderful world of Reiki. I did my level 1 and level 2 with the most amazing Reiki Master in the village where I lived and later my level 3. It was an intriguing start to my holistic journey, and in 2000, I decided that I wanted to do something else ultimately: I studied Reflexology and Indian Head Massage at a local college.

Moonbeam, furlough, and a gentle push in the right direction

In 1998 my daughter decided she would like to have riding lessons and was introduced to Moonbeam, a feisty little pony, who became my daughter's soul mate – however, he needed some TLC as he had some rather difficult habits. We tried everything to help alleviate his terror and fears but to no avail, until my Reiki Master told me about Bach Flower Remedies and an amazing lady in the village. A few days later we met and after a short conversation, she gave me a little bottle of wonderful remedies – with strict instructions. I duly administered them and within 3 days his fears seemed to diminish, his attitude changed, and he became much more relaxed. We completed the course of remedies and the fear never returned. He lived for another 18 years and died at the age of 43, in 2017. He gave me all I needed to know that Bach Flower Remedies were incredible, and I wanted to learn more.

My study of the remedies took me to the Bach Centre – the epicentre of my world – where the mother tinctures are still made, where Dr Bach lived, worked and died and where he gave so many people so much hope. In 2013 I became a practitioner, which gave me more opportunities to counsel and work with clients directly. I never dreamt that I would ever end up where I am now – working full time with them and helping to transform people's lives.

On 1 April 2020 I was furloughed from my corporate world, within 2 hours I had no communication with people I had known for 30 years, no corporate emails, no phone calls – all gone. I was stunned and also very lost. That afternoon my husband and I walked the dog across the village and chatted through my options, he said quite simply this is the opportunity to follow your dream. I needed that push to take myself off into a totally different world of networking and building different relationships.

Relationships and remedies

It seemed strange not to have my past with me, but I had to forge new relationships and move on. Thanks to a prior networking group I was part of, I was able to start and enter the new world of Zoom meetings and make new friends.

For me the networking was not about selling, it was a simple case of telling people about the remedies and talking about how they could help and how they would make life easier. In May 2020, I had a networking call with a group of 170 Bach Flower Practitioners from all across the world. We have Bach Practitioners in over 100 countries all around the world. The one common denominator between us all was that so few people know about the remedies, and it was so hard for us to get the message out about their properties and how people can benefit from them.

Covid-19 gave me the opportunity to help and talk to people and give them the remedies which in turn helped them. In some cases, they had miraculous benefits and in others they gave a beautiful opportunity of hope. It was a slow start, but the difficulties were surmountable and while finances were not at the top of the list, I was keen, if possible, to at least make a success of my work.

I knew the remedies would not let me down, but I needed to use the business ethics I had accumulated over time and entwine them with work I needed to do to create the remedy blends people needed.

Shock and trauma in a changing world

The first lesson was helping people overcome the shock and trauma of the first months of Covid-19. In my first week I spoke to a Managing Director who was losing his whole world and who was earning £10 per hour just to put food on the table – he was on the verge of suicide. His story was heart wrenching – he had remedies for no cost – however, I have had his appreciation back in spades with referrals.

I have heard some very sad stories over the last 18 months but bizarrely the story that sticks with me is that of my first client who came to me back in 2013 and explained that she had a fear of flying, and as it was a big birthday that year, her husband wanted to take her away and it meant flying. When I say frightened of flying, I mean terrified – she would hold her husbands' arms and make them bleed with the intensity of the hold. She and I talked through the fears and slowly over the next 6 months the story unfolded. Her fear of flying was linked to a fear of being sick and the fear of being sick went back to when she was abused by a family member when she was 10!! She had never told anyone about this. Over the months we laughed, we cried, we talked, and we had a hug; we used lots of tissues and spent lots of time in silence, but we made it. This beautiful young lady walked away from my front door 8 months later and said very quietly – "thank you for giving me the rest of my life back". What more did I need? It was a beautiful moment, and I knew I had to continue.

Covid and lockdown brought many more stories to my door, and situations that unravelled and resolved themselves on many occasions very easily.

I also helped an army veteran with PTSD; he had suffered greatly at the hands of his family when young and in order to get away had joined the army. Naturally in the army he solved one problem but of course had to brace himself for the tribulations that war – Iraq and Afghanistan – would hold for him. We have worked through all of the stories and discussed the remedies individually and last week when we spoke, he simply said "Eureka" – I have made it. He hadn't had a nightmare for 4 weeks, his spirits had lifted, he had stuck to the diet plan that he needed to follow, and he had managed to continue his exercises successfully for the last month – all of this had been a struggle for the last 5 months. We had chipped away at everything and each time the remedies had improved some things, but he had finally managed to put the whole thing together and felt complete. He was beaming and sitting more upright in the wheelchair and generally in the best shape since I had first met him.

Lockdown has been very cruel for so many people and I have so many stories to tell – the couple who were due to separate just before lockdown 1, he lost his job as a result of lockdown and couldn't leave, so for 18 months they have had to stay together and make it work – the remedies have actually eased the violence in the home, and although he's still leaving they are now friends, and it is workable.

The 72-year-old lady who would only leave home in daylight, who was terrified of doing anything at all, who had panic attacks frequently, in 5 months she had a part-time job, had come off her medication and was doing her own shopping and looking after her grandchildren – just pure joy!

At the beginning of lockdown, I was asked to help a young lad who was so shocked by lockdown and missed his friends so much he was devastated. He was also terrified for his grandparents and how they were going to manage – with the remedies we eased the situation for him. He is now feeling much happier with life and its returning to normal.

I also work with animals and have been asked to help with countless dogs over the period who have been delighted to see their owners at home but of course when lockdowns have ended, they have been left at home on their own to pine and whimper and in some cases destroy things around the house. They had no understanding of lockdown; they just thought their luck had changed because there was all this company – and when we all went back out again, they were quite perplexed. The remedies work wonders for separation anxiety, alleviate all the tension and allow the animals to settle down into the calm routine of life.

My journey over this last 2 years has been utterly amazing, from the corporate world to the job of my dreams working successfully with the Bach Flower Remedies and giving people back their lives – what more could I wish for. I have worked with young children helping them to sleep and a 93-year-old who wanted to die; I've worked with horses, dogs, cats and rabbits and all have left my services feeling better and calmer, enjoying life to the full. They have found a new side to life – one of calmness and balance and that feeling of being able to manage the emotions in a quiet and gathered manner. The remedies have a very subtle way of making you feel better – there is no suddenness to them. The beauty in the way that they work is quite remarkable.

Every day I thank Dr Bach for the work he did to give us these amazing remedies and for the beauty of the help that they give to my clients.

· · ·

BIO:

Ros Thompson is a Holistic Therapist, working mainly with Bach Flower Remedies. She is a married mum, with a beautiful daughter and a wonderful grandson to enhance her world. Ros works with the remedies to help ease negative emotions for people and animals, helping to ease their anxieties and fears, overwhelm, exhaustion, grief and other worrying concerns. The remedies help to make life easier one drop at a time.

www.remediesbyros.com

25

THE ROAD TO EXTRAORDINARY

Samantha Leith

I always knew I had 'it' in me. But what was it? Was it my ability to entertain, was it the way I organised parties, or I say gasping in horror, was it how I could break down a P and L? One thing was always certain, I was destined to do something. The drive for that was powerful. The other certainty was I was always going to be better off creating my own business to do whatever 'it' was.

My first paid job was singing. 50c for weddings and $1 for funerals. My mother would tell me to spend half and save half. Even in 1982 that was not a lot of money, so chances are it usually went on chocolate or something else to make me feel better. In hindsight, it was a hint that my road was going to involve personal development of some kind. I was always looking for things to help myself and others feel better!

As my childhood went on into my teen years my greatest moments were on stages, at parties, helping others and learning. These highlights made up for the drunken dramas at home and the trauma with a capital T, that we don't have time for in this chapter.

I was smart.
I was funny.
I was talented.
I was overweight.
I was broken.
I was entrepreneurial.

I would charge my friends $5 to come to my parties, then buy all the booze (we were mostly all underage, so do not tell my daughter) and make a healthy profit. I could put 200 people in a room having a great time as easily as I could colour coordinate my wardrobe. Yep, I was that kind of kid – still am.

When I was given the opportunity to tour with a band and leave school early, I took it. It horrified my teachers – they seriously expected me to do law, but I chose MC Hammer, dance parties and piano bars instead. What 17 year old wouldn't?

Sitting on pianos, telling stories, on stage in front of thousands, singing songs at theme parks – I always had one goal. To have someone in the audience laugh or cry, to think something, to feel something. I was home, I was me.

Touring my one woman show, singing interwoven with lessons of how the many layers of makeup tell the stories of our lives, should have been a dead giveaway for what I was made for, but alas, it still took longer to hit me.

I was Confident enough to do anything that was thrown at me, but I didn't have the Clarity to know exactly what I wanted to do, or the Courage to do whatever it was.

For years, I was what's known as a Sole Trader in Australia – this enabled me to maximise tax benefits etc of my multi passionate career. By the time I started my first 'real' company, I had done a plethora of things: studied accounting, been a national sales manager, hospitality, studied personal develop-ment and so much more. I was like a sponge trying to fill myself up, but it was partly because I had that voice in the back of my head reminding me constantly that I had to 'have something sensible to fall back on'. I mean really. Do I look like I wanted to study accounting? No offence to accountants, when they are passionate about it, they are amazing and we need them!

When I look back, these many careers and what I felt was my inability to 'finish' anything were all signs of my undiag-nosed ADHD (inattentive), but that's a whole other story!

My business, much like myself has 'pirouetted' over the years (I so can't say pivot anymore). I started as the financial controller for a couple of businesses, with a side hustle of a retail store (on and offline). This led me to helping people systematise their businesses through an online programme, coaching and speaking. Yep, I would stand there, usually in sparkles because I hadn't completely killed the showgirl inside, teaching people how to Ditch It, Delegate It, Leverage It and Live It.

The almost desperate (sometimes) need to help people that I had was a blessing and a curse. It led me to trying anything I could to help someone in business or life. It led me to being a people pleaser trapped in chains of servitude. It led me to wanting to get to the bottom of why we did what we did as humans. It led me to ignoring the bubbling dreams inside me. It led me to what I call the 'numb years'.

As a single mum to a 6 year old girl, I was hit with a heart-breaking trifecta. Within 6 months my father died, my brother died, and my mother had a massive stroke which resulted in her needing to live with my daughter and I. For the next 6 years, most decisions were made through the lens of what was best for my daughter and for my mother and her needs. It meant accepting any work that allowed me to be flexible and paying even less attention to the bustling chorus of my dreams inside.

I'm not alone in this. It's so common for women in particular to hide their desires in the dark while caring for or feeling responsible for others. Could I have gone for my dreams and looked after them? Probably, maybe. I'll never know. Don't get me wrong. Those years were incredible for many reasons, and I have no regrets. The health issues my mother had, forced me to look at my own health and get rid of 50kgs and my daughter is truly extraordinary.

As I came out the other side of those years. I had shed metaphorical baggage as well as physical. I'd shed unhealthy relationships and unrealistic expectations.

I could hear my voice.
I could acknowledge my dreams.
I could see a clear path to my greatest goal.

All of it. The good. The bad. The WTF. Led me to my business today. Led me to being who I am today, and I love who I am today.

I am worthy.
I am enough.
I am ready.

My business today is what it always has been at its core. Entertaining, Educating and Empowering people. It's who I've always been. I've simply done it under many differing guises.

I had a friend who has known me since those piano bar days say to me that I was always giving personal development talks. Interwoven between songs there would be a lesson of some kind.

Another friend recently told me that it didn't matter if it was a kids' party, or a small workshop she'd been to, I always entertained and made people feel special.

Finally a client and friend of mine reminded me that I was always encouraging people to better themselves through the power of continued education. That's the ultimate in empowerment.

I believe to my core that we all have the power to be Extraordinary.

I believe in people till they believe in themselves.

My business has been my second greatest teacher (my daughter being the first). I've loved it. I've hated it. I've been frustrated. I've been exuberant. I've been barely able to pay the bills. I've been triumphant at the end of some months. I've had some horrific failures. I've had award-winning successes. I've hired the wrong people. I've been stubborn and thought I could do it all myself. It's part of the course. All those things (and many more) are a part of running your own business.

Is having a business for everyone? Hell no! Don't ever get trapped in the belief that entrepreneurship is for everyone. It's simply not true. There are people that make amazing employees. If that's you. Be proud of that. The world needs you.

One of the most beautiful things about having your own business is that it can morph. It's unique, like you. Your DNA is yours alone, and so is your business. To copy another business is not only the wrong thing to do by them, it's the wrong thing to do by you!

During all those years where I was mentored and coached, studied and tried things, broke down and got back up, I never lost hope for one thing. That the penny would eventually drop. In fact I would say that when someone would question why I was attending or crewing another event or had signed up for another online course or challenge. My words were 'because today might be the day that I hear the one thing that makes the penny drop, and everything will change'.

Being open to the possibility of who you are and what you

are capable of. That's what separates so many of us. We all have so many possibilities. Are you open to yours?

My business has:

- Sold physical products that would help people to feel pampered
- Produced musical theatre that would help people to feel entertained
- Taught courses to start a business that would help people to feel accomplished
- Toured shows that would entertain and help the audience to feel alive
- Spoken to audiences to help them discover their passions and feel on purpose
- Provided accounting services that would help people to feel organised

And so much more. The common thread – helping people to feel something.

When I'm asked what my big why is, my answer in simple. To bring personal development to people that don't have a bookcase that looks like mine. Yes, that's a bit of a joke response, because humour is one of my natural go to's and well, because I have a 4m by 3m bookcase that's full of personal and business development and looks like The Home Edit colour coordinated the whole thing.

It's also real. When you have a business that's in the personal development space, we can easily take for granted what people have access to. We can think that everyone must know the basics of a success ritual or knows how to create their own talent stack. They don't. Millions of people have never heard of the books I have read multiple times or the leaders in this space.

If I spend the rest of my days opening people up to these possibilities through blending my singing and speaking, then not a day will have been wasted. If I can level the playing field of personal development by encouraging more women to stand out in the space, then I will have been part of great change.

It's personal development, but not as you know it.

BIO:

Keynote speaker, MC, Workshop Facilitator and Coach, Samantha Leith is a Woman on A Mission, helping people to become truly Extraordinary in their lives and workplaces, as leaders and in their teams. It's about developing the Confidence and Charisma needed to have people pay attention and building the Clarity and Courage needed to go after your dreams. She does this through her coaching programme How To Be Extraordinary and her onstage and offline keynote experiences, including The Sound of Empowerment – the personal development concert extravaganza. After 40+ years on stage (she started very young) she can be described as the imaginary love child of Bette Midler and Tony Robbins.

www.samanthaleith.com

26

HOW POWERFUL IS YOUR WHY?

Tara Day

My family are really precious to me. I imagine, especially if you have children, you are agreeing with me here.

This isn't an unusual feeling for mums generally and every child is a miracle, but I had to fight hard for mine which made wanting to be around to bring them up a massively important part of our decision making as a couple.

Married at 19 to a serving police officer who worked shifts for many years, I worked in early years and the caring sector with adults and children with severe behavioural problems and learning disabilities. I loved my jobs and the wonderful people I met and had the pleasure of supporting and working alongside, but ultimately I always wanted a family of my own.

The journey to becoming a mum

This proved to be a traumatic journey which resulted in three beautiful miracle babies.

To give you some perspective we tried for a family for five

years and eventually had to resort to medical help. We found
out we were expecting and were obviously thrilled. At the 20-
week scan we were informed that our baby wasn't growing
normally and was suffering from various abnormalities. We
were offered a second opinion and an abortion, but when we
asked if there was any danger to me or if the little one was
suffering, they said no. We decided to continue with the pregnancy, knowing that our little one wouldn't survive the birth.

We were supported emotionally by family and friends and
cared for by our church community. At 24-weeks and 1 day
(this proved to be hugely important and significant to us) our
firstborn, Elliot, arrived naturally and although still alive at the
start of labour, as expected he was stillborn.

Many horrific months followed of coping with a body that
had given birth but with no baby to hold and all the grief that
went with it. However, that one day of gestation over 24 weeks
meant that legally he was a stillbirth not a miscarriage which
meant by law he existed, and we were allowed to register his
birth and death and give him a funeral.

We held a funeral for him, and our church was packed. The
support, love, and prayers of our church community held us
together during and through that difficult time.

Roll on a year and I discovered I was pregnant again, naturally! A shock and a joy. As you can imagine, I was monitored
really closely, and as my obstetrician thought that Elliot's issues
were a one off, we didn't expect any surprises this time.

Cue my daughter Georgia arriving at 30 weeks absolutely
perfect, just tiny! We were thrilled, and she did really well and
came home after six weeks. We enjoyed our gorgeous little girl
while also hoping for a sibling. It took a while, but two and a
half years later we discovered I was expecting again. Monitoring was very frequent, but again my doctor didn't think there
was any cause for concern. When my son Cameron was born at
27 weeks as an emergency caesarean, our lives were turned

upside down once again, only this time we had a 3-year-old to factor in.

Due to his prematurity, he was transferred to another hospital further away and remained there until he was considered well enough to move back to the hospital he was born in. Travelling, visiting, and caring for our daughter was quite a feat. Thanks to amazing supportive friends and our church family we just about managed.

Cameron had to endure operations, sepsis, bleeds on his brain, ventilation and all the issues that came with it in a short space of time. But yet again, he defied the medical odds, and I brought him home two weeks before his due date – seriously tiny, with dodgy lungs but home. There we were with two incredible, healthy miracle babies, feeling seriously blessed and positive about our future as a family. Everyone who knew us thought this was probably a good time to be thankful and call it quits! I had other ideas and really wanted to complete the family with another baby. Was I crazy?

I discovered I was pregnant again then at the 12-week scan discovered this little one's heart had stopped. More loss and heartache but holding very tightly to our gorgeous two who were growing up healthy. Good time to stop? I still wanted a third, so we were thrilled to discover I was pregnant again a while later.

At this point there was serious concern that I would labour early again, but my doctor thought regular monitoring would be fine. I researched and believed I had a condition called incompetent cervix and asked for a stitch – this is a medical intervention to stitch your cervix up! The recommendation for having this procedure is between 10 and 12 weeks to lessen the risk of miscarriage. I pushed for a second opinion, and the second doctor took one look at my notes and said I needed the stitch. By the time it was arranged and preformed I was at 21 weeks and there was a huge risk of miscarriage. We both made it through, and I carried on with the pregnancy getting past first 27 then 30 weeks and hitting the unknown phase I hadn't yet experienced.

I grew enormous and along the way was diagnosed with gestational diabetes, injecting insulin four times a day. With this came the risk of extra fluid which would put the stitch at risk of bursting, so I was monitored closely and hospitalised a couple of times. I was booked in for an elective caesarean, so for the first time in five pregnancies I knew when I would give birth; it was almost laughable. Due to my diabetes, I was booked in for just after 38 weeks. This was between Christmas and New Year so midweek (Wednesday) was chosen and I told everyone exactly when I was having my baby.

Everyone found this really amusing and waited to find out whether I had a boy or girl. The only possible fly in the ointment was that due to my diabetes there needed to be a space in the neonatal unit in case the baby had low blood sugars.

We went in on the Wednesday but were home by the afternoon, as an emergency had come in and they couldn't accommodate us!! Can you imagine the reaction when friends and family were phoning my husband to find out how I was and ended up speaking to me still pregnant!! It's still a family joke now.

Our son Elijah arrived safely on the Friday, and it was like giving birth to and taking home a 3-month-old baby even though he was of very average weight. He stayed a night in special care and all the nurses and doctors who had cared for us twice before came to say hello which felt like the end of a long journey with friends.

Why am I telling you all this?

What does it have to do with being a businesswoman?

As I said at the beginning this is why I have always chosen work to fit around my family; they are so precious to us, and we always wanted me to be the one to be at home with them while my husband worked.

These life experiences taught me many things: resilience, strength of character, a positive mindset, and realisation that life is never straightforward!! It's true that challenges help you grow.

Opportunities and growth

Along came my first opportunity while the eldest two were little. I was invited to join a fairly new direct sales company to promote books and children's games. It was a family run company, and I loved reading to my two, so this worked out well.

I was able to bring some money to the family finances, have a bit of me time, and it was great for my confidence. As I spent the majority of my time with parents and young children, it was really popular and easy to sell. I made the parties fun and inter-active, and it gave us mums, particularly, a great social event to look forward to. We worked the timings around my husband's shifts, so it fitted in with family life and my children benefited from some wonderful books. Sadly the company chose to go back to selling to trade, but then I was offered the opportunity to join a local preschool, which worked out well with childcare as I took my youngest with me.

I left after 2 years and was offered the opportunity to join another company demonstrating and selling quality kitchen products. I really enjoyed this, having experienced running a business previously. I love cooking and baking and did well at it.

Then boom, I was diagnosed with breast cancer, having just turned 40 with three young children. Surgery, chemotherapy, and radiotherapy filled my next nine months, but I still kept my business going. Some of my close friends supported me by driving me to parties and doing all the lifting, while I did the demonstrating. This gave me something normal to focus on apart from my cancer and some me time again. Sadly, after I recovered and picked the business back up, the company withdrew from the UK, devastating many of us.

Shortly after this, I was offered the opportunity to join a company launching in the UK selling eco –friendly products for the home and body: Norwex. Becoming a founding member seemed like a sensible solution, and I began the journey with my current company. Their ethos and mission really spoke to me, as protecting the planet and reducing harmful chemicals in my home environment was high on my priority list! When you're part of a direct sales company, you're selling products on behalf of a company, but the business is yours to run how you want.

This way of working has been a huge part of my family life over the years and enabled me to be around for my children, build my confidence, contribute to family finances, and bring some amazing products into my home. Having flexibility has been so important to us, and I love that the result of these businesses has had a direct impact on my children. My daughter has grown up with a love of books and reading, gaining a first in her English literature degree, and my eldest son is doing hospitality and catering at college and working in a local pub kitchen. I am yet to see my youngest become an environmental expert but joking aside, they are now all more aware of harmful toxins and their impact on our health and environment.

I shall forever be grateful for the business opportunities offered to me and I hope you see that despite life's ups and downs, with a positive mindset, hard work and determination, anything is possible.

Your why may evolve along the way but always be sure of what is driving you and giving you purpose.

Is it easy?

No.

Is it a roller coaster?

Yes.

Is it hard work?

Definitely!

Is it worth it?

For all the reasons I've given, it's a yes from me.

Never be afraid to say yes when an opportunity is offered to you; you never know where it may take you.

BIO:

Tara Day is a proud mum of three amazing young people, wife, breast cancer survivor, and businesswoman. She has worked in full-time and part-time employment and benefited from a long career in direct sales. These have fed her passions and aligned with her values, grown her confidence and leadership skills, and given her lifelong friends. She is grateful to have just celebrated 10 years since her cancer diagnosis and is healthy and positive about her future.

www.taraday.norwex.eu

27

TOO MANY STRAWBERRIES IN
THE JAM

Victoria Schofield

Many great people have said many great things, but I am reasonably sure that no one ever said, "Go into lockdown, lose your job, sort out your loft and start a business!" Not really a cry of War Heroes!

Yet, I am rather proud of myself. Let me explain...

A friend of mine posted a message on Facebook thanking a local bakery for delivering an afternoon tea, in the first week of lockdown, to his Granny. My friend could not go to see her but the bakery went out of their way to help. The kindness and thoughtfulness of all involved struck a chord with me as I thought what if it was my Mum and Dad? My Aunty and Uncle? Would someone do the same for them? Later that day, reorganising the loft, as I suspect most people found themselves doing as we had nothing else more interesting to do, I found my Granny's china tea set and I started to join the dots. I could do something nice for people. I have a tea set, a cake stand and a car.

The Cup and Saucer was therefore born out of misfortune

or very good fortune and incredibly good luck when the rest of the country seemed to have neither. It is a very easy concept. I deliver beautifully presented teas to people on vintage crockery as a gift from other people. That is it.

Except, that it's not just it. It wasn't ever just it. There is slightly more to it. I deliver teas from people to people who are around the corner but can't or could not get there. I delivered and still am delivering from people to people who are isolating and are so upset and sad that they can't be there.

I catered for a funeral and my heart broke for the lovely lady who was just holding on as so many people could not be there. I cried all of the way home.

I have delivered teas from daughters and sons to their Mothers and Fathers from Canada, New Zealand, Australia, South Africa and America because they could not be there.

I have stood in the pouring rain yelling through a window just so that the person I was speaking to was actually speaking to someone for the first time in weeks.

I stood in the blistering heat watching a Victoria Sponge cake melt in front of my eyes as the recipient wanted to tell me all about her niece who had sent it to her.

I delivered on behalf of people who, during this pandemic, could not get to someone they loved. I was, and I remain, the conduit and a very happy conduit at that. This is my job. This is the point of The Cup and Saucer. That is the purpose of this business.

I am no angel. Believe me! I am not writing this to make you believe that I am. I am writing this to say there is a niche in every market. You just have to find it but you must love it and you must also be passionate about it.

Mistakes, I have made a few. Not many, thankfully, but when you do and inevitably will in a new business, fight all of your instincts to go into a darkened room and sob. Learn from it. Take a moment. Ask yourself did you actually do something wrong? Was your customer simply having a bad day themselves and you were the target? If it was your fault then fix it. Although how you fix the complaint that "there were too many Strawberries in the jam" still escapes me! Respond immediately is my advice. Deflate the situation. Say sorry even when it is not your fault. That is customer service and there is nothing more damaging than a bad review. So eating humble pie, or in my case a humble scone, is worth it.

Perfection. I am a control freak and a perfectionist so if a squished strawberry or raspberry appears on the vintage cake stands I drive away thinking "It's a total fail" Then I stop. Breathe and realise that there are two vital reasons why there may be a squished strawberry. First, you cannot make Clingfilm look elegant, despite my best efforts, trust me I have tried! Secondly, I would rather my clients are safe and so I have to wrap up everything to ensure. Raspberries bounce back!

I have had to learn to stop with the sackcloth and ashes routine. Not easy. I am a contract litigation solicitor by trade. I have spent most of my adult life arguing over where a comma or a full stop goes to ensure the safety of my client. I have stood outside of courtrooms trying not to throw up on my shoes (which were always fabulous by the way). This is a very different game but the same standards apply. If someone is paying you money, you provide an exceptional service. Full stop. However, no one will die, lose money or become homeless over a squished bit of fruit.

There is a saying that people eat with their eyes and I really believe it. You have one shot on the day. Present it to the client looking amazing. If it does not look great immediately, you have lost your crowd. Like an opening song at a concert. If the opening song does not move or excite you in the first few minutes you will be thinking why am I going to waste my time for the next hour and a half? Not everything that you do as a small business should be lovely, it has to be exceptional. Even when you are tired, even when you have had enough, and you are questioning the madness that made you set this business up, the product, your product must always look incredible. It is your name. It is your brand. You have chosen to do this so get on with it.

Mentioning the word brand... I have been advised repeatedly to branch out. "Think about platters." "Think about Supper Clubs." The thing is, I set this business up for a reason and it works. I love doing it. I am not a chef. There are far more qualified people than me to provide platters and Supper Clubs and they will do it sensationally better than I could. I deliver sandwiches, scones, cream, jam and cakes.

To begin a business this is all I can give you...

Learn everything that you can before you start. Everything. Every rule, every regulation.

Take courses. Get the qualifications. You would be surprised how many of them are free or inexpensive but so worthwhile. Listen to every single word they say. I spent six virtual hours on my GNVQ (General National Vocational Qualification) food and hygiene course, Grade Two. I then had to take the two hour virtual exam but I danced around my living room with pride when minutes later I passed! An achievement. A first tiny step. I printed out my certificate and framed it!

Social media is your best friend! It takes hours but worth it. Take a picture of everything you create or do. I have moved lights and fallen off ladders to get the right shot! Alternatively employ someone to do it for you. It will be money very well spent. Be mindful of the fact that people check their phones at various times during the day. So target your market. First thing in the morning, lunchtime, early evening. About bedtime. Think about when you look at your phone. Ask yourself what you are looking for and why and when?

Get a website properly set and update it as often as you can with photographs of your product.

My Business Google is a fabulous way to get reviews and hits to get as many Google hits as you can. It will make a huge difference as it pops you up on the Google search stakes.

My lovely dad pointed out to me, when I was writing this chapter, that without lockdown and without losing my job The Cup and Saucer would never have been created. Therefore, two life changing events made me an independent businesswoman.

Will it be a storm in a teacup? Will it fail? Who knows? However, I would like to think that it will continue. If nothing else, I have been allowed to believe that I am a success and I have achieved something a little bit fabulous.

Without the enduring support of my family, Mum, Dad, Beccy, Ben and friends, I could not have done this. I thank you all.

This is, however, dedicated to Marc, my husband, without whom I would never have had the belief that I could. Thank you and I love you x

BIO:

Victoria Schofield is the founder and owner of The Cup and Saucer. It is a little over one year old.

She is 42 years old and was born and raised in Sunderland. Victoria went to Essex University where she studied law and then lived in London for 17 years working as a commercial litigation solicitor. She moved to Winchester, Hampshire just over 8 years ago and worked as a consultant for the NHS.

Victoria is married to Marc and has Margot, a Cavalier King Charles spaniel. The naughty but nice company mascot.

She loves travelling, cooking, baking, reading and photography. She loves people, fascinating creatures.

www.thecupandsaucer.co.uk

28

FROM MUSCLING THROUGH TO FINDING FLOW

Manon Swaving

This is a story about progress, not perfection. I started my own business because I wanted to work in alignment with my purpose and support people to bring all of who they are into the world with clarity, joy and ease. I never intended to be a businesswoman, I just needed a formal structure so people could pay me for what I loved doing and to make sure everything was legal and I paid taxes. It took me more than 10 years to get to this point and my journey starts with my first job...

Four years into my first job at Unilever, I realised this is not what I'm meant to be doing. I switched careers in my late twenties and found my purpose in supporting others through personal development. I trained and coached with different companies; I learnt on the job from one of the best trainers and coaches out there. It was challenging, fun and meaningful.

After a few years of facilitating overnight-trainings all over the country, having two babies and a husband who was hustling to get his partnership within a big firm, I realised something needed to change.

I was burnt out and unhappy. I wasn't walking my talk. After my maternity leave I chose not to go back to work as a trainer and left one of the most inspiring training companies in the Netherlands.

Although I'm grateful we had enough funds for me not to work, I struggled. Motherhood and especially parenting turned out to be one of the hardest things I've done in life. The love part of this job flowed naturally from my heart. But the repeated chores, the patience, the consistency and the planning that is required brought out the worst in me. I truly suck at it and I felt shame and guilt about not being able to do it well.

I'm a good mother and I absolutely love my kids, but if I had a boss at that point in time I would have probably been fired! I wasn't the best version of myself. I had hoped that staying home with the children would help my husband and I grow closer together but we actually drifted apart even more.

What do I feel? What do I want?

A year later, while sitting in the playground snapping at my 4 year old for throwing sand in his sister's eyes, I asked myself two questions: "what do I feel?" and "what do I want?". The answer was shockingly simple: I feel bored and I want to go back to work.

I started volunteering as support staff at a coach training company. I got support from my husband and a fantastic babysitter and wiggled myself out of the full-time mom-job.

I loved it. I blossomed and soon enough I was at the Chamber of Commerce to set up my company so I could get paid for what I loved doing. First as a facilitator, then as co-lead and finally as lead trainer and creator of the programme we ran twice a year.

My patience with my little ones grew, my smiles were more

authentic and the chemistry between me and my man came back.

I learnt a lot as a result of teaching people to become professional coaches and facilitating them in their personal journey. This was one of those jobs I could only succeed at when I was 100% practising what I preached. Every time I led the training, I was a student all over again! I spiralled up: I grew, those I worked with grew, my rates grew, the business grew.

I was at my best until one day my husband came home and said: "we are moving to Singapore." In other words: "please leave what you have carefully built in the last three years behind and start over in a country where you don't know anyone."

I welcomed the adventure and living abroad excited me, yet mixed emotions ran through my body when I heard this message. The idea of becoming an expat wife was far from appealing to me. I noticed a lot of internal judgement and fear about becoming one myself.

Three months later, in the middle of a coach training I was leading, I said goodbye and flew off with my family to Singapore. There I was back into the full-time mom-job I had worked so hard to wiggle myself out of.

Turning my side hustle into my business

It took a year to get used to the hot climate, settle the kids in school and find new friends. People asked me to join tennis competitions, volunteer at the charity associations and support the school library on Wednesday mornings. All wonderful suggestions and noble things to spend time on but none of them brought a sparkle to my eyes.

The best option for me was to recreate the work I had done in the Netherlands. I signed a licence to conduct the coach training in Singapore but just as I was ready to set up my own business – I found out the rules had changed. Setting up a simple sole proprietorship was off the table. Now I needed to bring in serious money, foreign investors and fill in complicated forms to get a business permit. I hired a lawyer to support me, spent lots of money, filled in many forms and my application to set up a business was turned down by the Singapore government. I hired another company to support me, spent even more money, filled in more forms and again my application was rejected.

Clearly, this was not the way forward for me. But I was stubborn and muscled through.

I was invited by the founders of the coach training company to facilitate with them in Thailand. Since the work was outside of Singapore, I could do this without having my own business. I flew back and forth to Bangkok, enjoyed the adventure, loved the work and met interesting people.

I continued to work unpaid in Singapore. I created the transformational workshops I loved doing, flew in a team from the Netherlands to help facilitate and somehow found ways to legally do all this. It worked but it felt like it was an uphill battle.

In the meantime I noticed more and more women were gathering around me. After the birth of my second baby I attended a women's circle. What I thought to be a relaxed retreat turned out to be a full on 5-day transformational experience that changed my life.

I kept yearning to be in circle with women but couldn't quite find one I felt I belonged. So I flew back and forth to Europe learning about feminine embodiment circles, with the intention to create them myself.

One day I got a phone call from Danielle asking if I wanted to hold a feminine embodiment circle for the women in her new moon lodges. Danielle had built a beautiful community of conscious women in Singapore and I was utterly moved by her generous gesture to open her doors to launch my offering. It was the first time I facilitated a women's circle. I felt scared and excited at the same time.

Things started to grow organically from there. Moving from circles at home with two friends, to renting a place and charging a small fee to cover the costs. Gorgeous groups of women started forming and things started to flow.

Combining my skill for holding a transformational space with my passion for feminine embodiment turned into a magical offering and I wasn't the only one who longed for this. I chose to let go of teaching coaching and brought all of my attention to the circles.

Although I was passionate about feminine embodiment and clear about my purpose for bringing more feminine energy into this world, I never thought of turning the circles into a business.

Then my dad passed in October 2020. I flew back to the Netherlands to say goodbye, organise the funeral and sell my childhood home, while my family stayed in Singapore. It was a raw and difficult time. While I was in my two-week hotel-room-quarantine in Singapore it hit me: life is too short to do what you love as a side hustle. If I was to take myself seriously and really make a difference with my gifts, I'd better up my game and change my self-limiting beliefs that *running a business is a hassle* and *I'm not a businesswomen*.

One morning during those two weeks in quarantine, I woke up with a clear message: "I'm investing $10K in my business and will turn into $100K by the end of 2021." Now this was not so much about the numbers for me. For the first time I allowed myself to think big and lean into a whole new chapter.

I invested in a business coach, an enthusiastic and skilled Crazy Daisy woman named Trudy Simmons. She inspired me to set meaningful goals and held me accountable.

I gathered my courage and hired legal support to set up my own company in Singapore once more and succeeded. Three times really is a charm!

I invested in a designer who created a super charged sigel as my logo and while doing so, challenged me about my clients. G – who's non-binary – made me realise that some of my circles are women circles and some are not. I opened up the majority of my circles for everyone who wants to awaken their feminine energy, regardless of gender. Instantly I felt more alignment with my purpose. G also nudged me to use my own name as my company name, which required me to fully own my gifts and magic. Again, I was invited to take my own medicine.

I invested in my website, which I tried and failed to create myself in the past two years. Vicky not only got the job done beautifully but she also patiently helped me get over my tech phobia and taught me how to use all the techy-back-end programs. Every time I receive a Thrive cart confirmation email with the title 'congratulations you've made a sale!', my heart jumps.

I now create online and offline offerings. My clients can register, donate and pay through my website and receive beautiful looking, automated confirmation emails. This may not seem like a big deal to some, but this is what truly enabled me to step into thinking big and leaning in.

All of this I created during lockdowns while home schooling kids, navigating Covid restrictions and other sticky stuff. Sometimes I felt I didn't make any progress, but looking back now I made quantum leaps.

My learnings

Doing what I love allows things to flow with ease.

Owning my gifts changes the flow into a stream.

Turning my gifts into a business creates the possibility for the stream to become a mighty river.

And investing in good support is gold and pays back.

. . .

Recently, I received a testimonial from a participant who said "these circles are a sacred space for women to safely open up, grow, have fun and weave threads of love together."

I love my business!

BIO:

Manon Swaving is a professional ICF certified coach, facilitator and magic maker who loves nature, dance and photography. She currently lives in Asia with her husband and two kids. She holds a bachelor's degree in event marketing and is educated in group dynamics, family constellations, feminine embodiment and Reiki.

She believes the world needs more feminine energy. Many of us, regardless of gender, rely heavily on our masculine side to get things done quickly and we've lost touch with our feminine within which is our source of life energy and inspiration. Through her work she supports those who want to awaken their feminine energy and bring all of who they are into the world with clarity, joy and ease.

www.manonceciel.com

29

THE IMPORTANCE OF BEING
DISCONTENT

Angela Raspass

Perhaps you've opened this chapter because of an increasing sense of discontent and yearning that's becoming difficult to ignore. Your Next Chapter is calling you.

One of the most valuable ways you can channel your experience is through the lens of a business. It allows you to focus your sense of purpose, to contribute, to create, and enjoy deep fulfilment, making a difference in the lives of others. You might be drawn to entrepreneurship for the first time, or perhaps you have an existing business you're looking to revitalise, realign, expand or let go of so you can move more in the direction that's calling you now. You're in good company. Brené Brown says it so well – "Midlife is when the universe gently places her hands upon your shoulders, pulls you close, and whispers in your ear: I'm not screwing around anymore. Use the gifts you were given!".

When we consciously choose to step into our Next Chapters with focus and anticipation, ready to be challenged and stretched, life becomes full. Our spirits soar. That feeling of flatness recedes, replaced by what I have come to call "Joy Jolts", delicious, sudden infusions of intensely positive emotions that fill your body, mind and soul right to its edges. I want more of those. And I want them for you too. I want you to begin to imagine what's possible for you too, as you expand fully into the woman you are becoming.

So where do you begin?

I developed the Next Chapter Change Cycle after making sense of my own journey and then helping many of my clients navigate the same journey. The model has two stages – the Deliberation stage, which encompasses discontent and desire and the Doing stage, which comprises design and delivery of your ideas. The two stages are intersected by a decision and at each step we need to be aware of the interference caused by doubt, uncertainty, fear and misbeliefs.

When we view discontent as an invitation to explore something new, its purpose is positive. It can be really useful to get us moving when it's grounded in curiosity and possibility, providing us with energy and enthusiasm to seek growth and new ideas. Discontent is the launchpad for significant change, fuelling you with inspiration and motivation.

But it can also have a darker side.

If a sense of discontent is generated through watching other people's lives on social media and other unfair surface level comparisons, a general sense of "not enoughness", disappointment and even resentment can appear and when this happens, inspiration and action are unlikely side effects.

To avoid this, put on your glass blinkers and focus inside to find your truth with discernment and critical awareness.

How did the model play out for me?

When I look back, two powerfully significant experiences stand out for me, both born in deep discontent.

The first actually took place in 2006, but its roots were in the mid-eighties when I was a teenager. Back then, I tried so hard to fit in, but managed to stand out in all the ways that adolescents abhor. I'd always been a "swat" at school. For non-New Zealanders, that means I studied hard, did well and was liked by teachers and dismissed by most of the "cool crowd". I was also rather physically uncoordinated, with poor eyesight that meant I was the quintessential last to be picked for softball and netball teams, the key sports of the era.

But then I discovered I could run and, fortunately, you don't need 20:20 vision for that. Athletics became my new favourite thing, and I could not have been more elated when, as a 13-year-old, one soaring leap into the long jump pit nabbed me the gold medal at the North Island School Championships. This achievement capped off a fabulous year alongside a few academic prizes and I was practically bouncing with pride when I walked on stage in front of 1350 kids.

Until the hissing began.

The low hum of disapproval started somewhere in the middle of the assembly and spread across the crowd until it felt like the entire hall was alight with disapproval and rejection. My heart was thumping erratically. I could feel my pulse in my ears, deafening me. I disconnected from my body and yet somehow, made it across the stage. In that moment all of my suspicions about myself were confirmed. I was inherently wrong, completely flawed, utterly unworthy.

This primary experience of acute shame shaped me, defined me and over time, almost broke me. When your self-image feels eroded at the core, the pain of that disconnection can be so acute that your survival demands anaesthesia of some sort. In my case, I chose alcohol for my self-medication and steely determination, achievement and external approval for my self-esteem.

This was the combination that saw me able to soldier on and achieve many "tick the box" goals and successes on the outside – a great career, marriage, children and my own small business, but by my mid-thirties, the physical and emotional cost of maintaining the mask of external confidence and achievement became too high. I was trapped in the cycle of being internally numbed by addiction and externally chained to a chameleon-like existence to ensure the approval of others.

I searched for answers, for an escape route. I knew there had to be another way to live. Simple discontent had exploded into desperation, but I was exhausted and close to giving up. I'd explored too many options to help me to escape from the grip of my addiction. From the teeth gritting, nail-biting agony of determined abstinence through sheer willpower, to visiting health farms and sporadic counselling, to importing herbs and subliminal CDs that were "guaranteed to free me".

Nothing worked because I was never truly honest. Shame wouldn't allow me to be.

While I did manage to maintain the role of wife and mother, putting one foot in front of the other, in a state referred to as "high functioning alcoholism" by addiction specialists, the colour had drained from my life. I was submerged in fear, unable to see a way out, terrified that the cracks would begin to show in the careful façade I had in place and that the world would soon see me as I really was.

Somehow, thank god, my story took a turn. One night in late 2006 I was alone in my home, my family asleep upstairs. I was in the bathroom, looking in the mirror, groundhog day nipping at my heels, my Inner Critic, circling. But for some reason, this time in the quiet of the night, something shifted. I remember it vividly. For the first time in as long as I could remember, I clearly saw my pain. I saw my sorrow. I saw my heart. And I softened for a moment. Just long enough for the thought to slip in that I could try asking for help and possibly, just possibly, leave this dark place. I now know that the internal voice I connected with that evening was a part of me I've learnt to call the Inner Sage. She is the essence of each of us. Timeless. Patient. Loving. She is also discreet, and often hard to discern under the noise, bluster and discouragement of your inner critic. Sometimes you need to let go to connect with her. You need to actually stop. To pause and listen. I was still and quiet enough to hear her that night.

Two weeks later I was in short-term rehab, beginning a twelve-step programme that heralded an amazing new chapter of my life. I'm now in my fifteenth year of continuous recovery and have a completely revitalised mindset. Self-loathing has been replaced by self-compassion, an unconditional, supportive friendship with myself and a deep appreciation of and reconnection to my unique, unquestionable, boundless worth. I've often shared in recovery meetings that alcohol hijacked me, it took me off my path for several years, but now I'm back again, becoming the woman I've always been meant to be, with a depth of empathy and insight that I may never have developed without this experience.

Another chapter unfolds

My second turning point was in 2012. I had just arrived at the airport to pick up my husband after the Sydney to Lord Howe Island Yacht race. Graham jumped into the car and tossed his sail bag onto the back seat. Eyes shining, a huge grin on his face, his excitement was tangible.

"It was just incredible! Amazing! One night I was on evening watch and the sky was perfectly clear. The moon illuminated the ocean, the water was shimmering, it was the most beautifully calm experience. You're just surrounded by open ocean and then there's the

moment when the island comes into sight on the horizon, it just takes your breath away".

My husband was stepping into his own Next Chapter. A career of management consulting was giving way to the world of sailing, and he had recently begun a business in the industry. As he shared his stories of the adventure, his first off-shore race, I could feel my own tension increasing. My heart was hammering in my chest, my stomach was in knots, and I was finding it hard to breathe through the simmering resentment that was gripping me.

Finally, he turned to me and innocently asked "so, how was your week?" I promptly burst into tears and smacking my palms against the steering wheel in frustration cried "I just don't think I can do it anymore".

I'd built my Marketing Agency, Ideas Into Action from my dining room table with small children underfoot into a thriving small business, operating from an office we'd bought on Sydney's North Shore, with a small team of full-time staff and fabulous suppliers. We were taking care of diverse clients across three states, enjoying increasing brand recognition in the market and generating that magical multiple six figures in revenue. If so many of the success boxes were ticked, then why did I feel so miserable, exhausted and utterly, miserably discontent?

Perhaps if I'd looked a little closer at my reliance on cigarettes and energy drinks, the crazy juggle of before and after school care, the late nights and early mornings, the trying to be all things to all people – the very best mother, wife, employer and business owner I could be, leaving very little time for me, I might have seen this outburst just waiting to leap onto the stage.

When Graham put his hand over my mine and quietly said.

"So, don't" I looked sharply at him in disbelief. Surely it wasn't that simple?

Just because you can do it doesn't mean you should

Something inside of me cracked open that day and over the next few months I finally made the choice to close the business, let go of my staff and shift from business consulting to mentoring. These days I understand that a sustainable business is one that blends contribution, fulfilment and financial reward. All three need to be present in your next chapter. That's the business I have now, and I delight in helping other women to also appreciate the value of their own unique experience and insights, to trust their intuition and realign their business vision and services with their values, not just their skills.

And so, I invite you to embrace discontent, to listen to what is calling you, and step forward with a fiercely beating heart, inspired by your desire to make a difference in your own next chapter.

BIO:

Angela Raspass is a Sydney-based business mentor, author, and self-worth educator with a particular passion for supporting women to step into their next chapter and do the work in the world they're here for. In 2020 she published "Your Next Chapter – Ditch your doubt, own your worth and build the business you *really* want" which is available from her website.

www.angelaraspass.com

30

CHARMED GROWTH

Lisa Erricker

I've never been very good at gardening. Or cooking. I always wore high heels everywhere from the age of 16. So naturally, in 2019, I thought it would be a great idea to buy a farm...! But I'm getting ahead of myself.

I'm supposed to start at the beginning – always a good place to start, right? But I'm honestly not sure I can even remember exactly when I started my first business, or precisely how I started. As with life in general, while it would be lovely to look back on a neat set of steps or stages that show where I've come from to where I am now (and indeed, where I'm going next), my experience hasn't been neat. It hasn't been linear. But that's also been a big part of the fun.

What I can tell you is that I have always been crafty – in the creative sense of the word! As far back as I can possibly remember, I've kept myself busy creating and crafting things. School holidays were spent drawing, fashion designing, or making origami flowers. Birthdays and Christmases usually involved a new craft kit of some kind – I remember rushing to finish the cross stitch kit my grandparents bought me one Christmas in time to show them for New Year. I guess I grew up in quite a creative family. No one in the family made a living from crafting, but there was always a project to do at the weekend, and I was always encouraged to make things.

Entrepreneurial seeds

The idea of selling the things I made was seeded quite early. My dad did the odd craft stall occasionally, and he was a governor at my infant school, so my parents were always involved with setting up the school fairs. Packing a paste table and a float of rattling change into the car never felt abnormal – it was just another weekend activity. So, making the leap in my teens to booking my own craft stalls didn't seem like a big deal.

That first big decision though, in booking my own craft stalls, was prompted by two things – both quite simple really. Firstly, I was a teenager who wanted to earn more money. I had a part-time job in retail while at college and university, but what teenager doesn't want a bit more cash to spend on nights out and new shoes? Secondly, my love of crafting was resulting in the build-up of a big stash of stuff. All the crafters out there will relate to the ever growing boxes and piles of 'stuff'. As much as I was into lots of different crafts, jewellery making was beginning to take over as the favourite, and there are only so many pairs of beaded earrings and braided bracelets that you can wear yourself or give to your friends and family. I needed a way to get rid of some of the things I'd made and to make room for more – trying to sell seemed like a great solution.

So, by the time I was in my early twenties, I had a hobby that mostly paid for itself. I carried on making things because I enjoyed it. It was simply what I liked to do with my spare time.

Then, every now and again, I would book a craft stall some-where local and sell a few things. I learnt a lot during that time – I gained a lot of confidence with face-to-face selling and setting up stalls, but also learnt about which items sold best, and what I enjoyed doing most … which was working with charms.

A charming passion

Making charm jewellery hits all my buttons. I love researching new themes and product ideas, finding out which charms are out there that I can use. I love how bloomin' cute they are! And I love putting the designs together, choosing which bead styles and colours to add. Creating charm jewellery gives me the constant variation and creativity that I know I crave in my life – there's always a new theme to explore. More than anything though, I love how personal charm gifts can be for the recipient – there is absolutely nothing better than having someone look at your stall and excitedly spot a charm bracelet they love, because it tells a story that means something to them.

Even though I was selling at this point, I didn't really consider my jewellery-making to be a proper business, or myself to be a proper businesswoman. It was definitely just a hobby. After all, I got a full-time teaching job after university, so I was a teacher, wasn't I? A teacher with a hobby for the holidays? That was how I identified.

Something had to give

I can pinpoint when that way of thinking began to change, and I knew I wanted to make it more than just a hobby. Again, there are two things that I can think of that prompted the change. The first was that after a few years of full-time teaching, I began to recognise that I was suffering with stress. My husband, who was also a full-time teacher, was also suffering with stress. I've always been one to burn the candle at both ends anyway, but teaching can be an all-consuming career, and it was slowly making both of us unwell. For the benefit of our mental health, I knew I needed to find a way to make a living, or at least part of a living, that wasn't in teaching. I didn't actually want to give up teaching – I still don't and am still teaching now. It's a job I love in so many ways. But I needed some flexibility. If I could find a way to teach part time, but still be able to pay my mortgage and bills, then life would still be busy, but a more manageable sort of busy. A more enjoyable busy. A less-danger-ous-to-my-health sort of busy.

I didn't need a way out of teaching entirely, but I did need to know it was possible to do other things, and not be 'just' a teacher with slowly declining mental health. Strangely, even then, despite my experience with craft stalls and jewellery making, I wasn't sure that running a more serious business was the answer. But I searched around for some support and came across a new group on social media, the Hampshire Women's Business Group. I posted a few times about my 'hobby', and one day completely out of the blue, Trudy gave me a call. It was just to chat really, to find out more about me, my charm jewellery, and where I wanted to take my business … and there it was. Someone was actually talking to me about growing my busi-ness. Someone who didn't know me as a teacher, or a hobbyist, but saw the potential for a real business.

Of course, after I put the phone down, my friends and family were as supportive as always and said they knew I could do it. I've always been very lucky to have support and encouragement at home. But this was different, because someone from the world of business had told me it was possible, and all of a sudden, I believed it too. It was possible, and it was what I needed. It was a way forward.

Learning and growth

It hasn't been a quick or easy process to build my business since that phone call. I've had plenty of weeks, even months, when life has been busy, and I haven't been able to give my business the attention it needed to grow. But in between those times, I've made small steps forward – I've reached out to other local businesswomen for help with a logo, branding, and packaging. I've attended some workshops on social media advertising. I'm constantly updating and refreshing my product photography and keeping my selling platforms updated. I'm not an expert in any of these things, but I have little by little invested in an event here and there to help me learn at a comfortable pace. I've learnt to live by the philosophy that even a small step is still a step forward, and I'm getting better at asking for help when I need it. I'm used to being the teacher, but in growing my businesses, learning has been key.

Charm Bound is now a business that helps me make a living. Notice I said business, not hobby?! It's not my full-time job, but it is a real business, and it has meant that both my husband and I can now teach part time. I still love teaching – in fact, going part time has helped me find joy in being in the classroom again. That's pretty special as it is, and I could probably wrap up my chapter here with my business happily ticking along, and a lovely happy ending about finding balance and having belief in yourself or something along those lines. But I said at the beginning that my story has not been neat. There's a plot twist coming.

A different kind of growth

In 2019 we bought a smallholding. 'Hang on', you may be thinking. 'What, now? She runs a jewellery business, where does the farm appear from?' It wasn't a move I expected to make, but a property came on the market, and we saw an opportunity.

Both my husband and I love the countryside, and so a rural cottage with land was a dream. We had talked about retiring to the country in the distant future, keeping animals and growing our own food. My parents-in-law were looking for a project, and this property had a barn ready for conversion. None of us had expected to find those things there and then, but it seemed to be the right fit for us, and so we went for it.

We have big dreams for this place. Dreams of chickens, goats, and pigs. Dreams of growing flowers and food. Dreams of a craft studio, of offering workshops and wellbeing sessions. There is so much that I want to do here, and I'm lucky to have this opportunity to be able to continue to grow, both personally and professionally, in this new direction. It seems strange, in a way, to be writing a chapter for a book about running a business, when in many ways I feel that I have barely started, and that the best of my business is yet to come. What I do know though, is that there is no way I would have had the confidence to embark on this new adventure were it not for all the steps I'd taken before, and everything I'd learnt along the way.

I think that many of us are taught from a young age that we need to pick a career. That we have certain things that we are good at, and that we learn our trade, and then we stick with it. By far the most important lesson I've learnt through experience, however, is that it's ok to change, and it is more than ok to keep learning. My skills and my interests have evolved over time, and my business can too. That doesn't mean that my business story is a messy one. It means that it is a real one, that has grown and changed and evolved with me as I gain experience and learn new things. My business story doesn't have a clear beginning, it has a very meandering middle, and I am nowhere near the end. I can't wait to see what happens next.

BIO:

Lisa is a teacher, crafter and business owner from Portsmouth. She is currently living on a smallholding on the Isle of Wight with her husband, dog, multiple (and multiplying) chickens, and big dreams of more mad adventures to come.

www.instagram.com/littlehouseonthewight

ABOUT THE DAISY CHAIN GROUP

Trudy Simmons started The Daisy Chain Group in 2010. It was started to support and encourage businesswomen to have a safe space to share their journeys, and to be seen and heard in their endeavours.

Since its inception, the concept has grown to include platforms for women to find their voice and become more visible in lots of different ways. Whether it is attending The Crazy Daisy Networking events to grow your audience, coming along to The Spectacular Online Business Symposium to learn from world class speakers from around the globe, Make the opportunity to speak at The Spectacular to share your wisdom, be a part of the Shine On You Crazy Daisy book series to share your story, or be on the Shine On You Crazy Daisy Podcast to give your story gravitas and hear it in your own voice.

The Daisy Chain Group also offers The Accountability Club for businesswomen to work out how to build momentum and consistency in their businesses by deciding where their challenges are, how to overcome them and what they are committing to for the next 2 weeks - this is GOLD if you are a procrastinator (I see you!), or if you want to grow your business.

The Accountability Club is direct help and support from Trudy with her no BS way of cutting through the challenges and being able to find the next action steps to help you to move forward.

Trudy is known for her engaged communities on Facebook - The Hampshire Women's Business Group (for local business-women) and The International Women's Business Group (for any businesswoman that wants or has a global audience).

HAVING FUN in your business is a core value of The Daisy Chain Group. Having fun and TAKING ACTION is what builds you AND your business.

You can find The Daisy Chain Group here: www.thedaisy-chaingroup.com

https://www.facebook.com/daisychaingroup

https://www.instagram.com/daisychaingroup/

https://www.linkedin.com/in/trudysimmons/

You can find The Daisy Chain Group communities here: https://www.facebook.com/groups/hampshirewomens-business

https://www.facebook.com/groups/internationalwomens-business

You can find our services here:

The Crazy Daisy Networking

https://www.thedaisychaingroup.com/crazy-daisy-networking-club

The Accountability Club

https://www.thedaisychaingroup.com/the-accountability-club

You can find the Shine On You Crazy Daisy Podcast here: https://www.thedaisychaingroup.com/podcasts/shine-on-you-crazy-daisy

EVERY TIME YOU BUY FROM A SMALL BUSINESS, THEY DO A HAPPY DANCE!

As we gain, so can we give.

10% of the profits from this book will be donated to Healthcare Workers' Foundation Family Fund. The fund will support the children and families of healthcare workers who have passed due to Covid-19. To donate and/or support this incredible charity, please go to this link – https://gofund.me/8aed0fc3

OTHER BOOKS

AVAILABLE NOW

Shine On You Crazy Daisy – Volume 1

Available on Amazon, iBook and in all good bookshops.

COMING SOON

Shine On You Crazy Daisy – Volume 3

Available in November 2021 – more stories, more inspiration, more motivation to get out there and do what you WANT to do with your business. We are all in this together.

Printed in Great Britain
by Amazon